Biafra and the Nordic Media

Biafra and the Nordic Media

Witness Seminar with Uno Grönkvist, Lasse Jensen, Pierre Mens, and Pekka Peltola

Norbert Götz & Carl Marklund (eds)

Issues of Contemporary History / Samtidshistoriska frågor

The Institute of Contemporary History /
Samtidshistoriska institutet (SHI)
Södertörns högskola
SE-141 89 Huddinge

shi@sh.se
www.sh.se/shi

© The editors

Cover Image taken in Biafra, August 1968, courtesy of Pierre Mens
Cover: Jonathan Robson
Graphic form: Per Lindblom & Jonathan Robson

Stockholm 2024

Issues of Contemporary History /
Samtidshistoriska frågor nr 48
ISSN: 2004-8858
ISBN: 978-91-89615-48-9

Contents

Introduction

The Biafra crisis, also known as the Nigerian Civil War, which unfolded from 1967 to 1970 garnered immense global attention. The expressions "Children of Biafra" or "Biafran Babies" became a symbol for how the West perceived Africa. A decisive factor for the commitment to Biafra was the media coverage, with images of malnourished children galvanizing calls for urgent and concrete intervention from the global community. Reports detailing famine and human suffering mobilized Nordic civil society. Church aid organizations, national Red Cross societies, Save the Children and special Biafra committees organized relief efforts in solidarity with Biafra and its distressed civilian population.

Despite the pleas from civil society for assistance, there was no uniform understanding at various political levels. The secession of Biafra not only threatened the Nigerian nation state but also challenged the post-colonial world order. The absence of United Nations (UN) support for intervention in the Biafra crisis underscored the moral and political complexities of decolonization, leaving a lasting imprint on humanitarian crises in the so-called Third World for decades to come. The extensive humanitarian airlift organized by global civil society saved lives. But it also inadvertently prolonged a bloody civil war – a difficult moral dilemma that persists to this day.

Drawing on our previous research on humanitarian aid in the Nordic countries and the wider world,[1] the project "Civil Society

---

[1] Carl Marklund, *Neutrality and Solidarity in Nordic Humanitarian Action* (London: Overseas Development Institute, 2016); Carl Marklund, "From Unconditional Solidarity to Conditional Evaluability: Competing Notions of Conditionality and the Swedish Aid Model," in Antoine de Bengy Puyvallée and Kristian Bjørkdahl (eds.), *Do-Gooders at the End of Aid: Scandinavian Humanitarianism in the 21st Century* (Cambridge: Cambridge University

without Boundaries: Nordic Humanitarianism Facing the Biafra Crisis" (BIAFRA), funded by the Swedish Research Council, examines how Nordic civil society responded during the Biafra crisis. Hosted by the Institute of Contemporary History at Södertörn University and led by Professor Norbert Götz, the project's team includes researchers Susan Lindholm and Carl Marklund, along with Martin Johansson, who is supported by a special grant from the research programme Reimagining Norden in an Evolving World (ReNEW), funded by NordForsk.

The project aims to chart the perceptions and actions of contemporary civil society organizations, media, and politicians. It seeks to understand how these entities perceived their own roles, as well as those of others. The focus extends to their views on those in need of assistance and how they portrayed their commitment, not only in relation to Biafra and Africa but also in the broader decision-making dynamics between the global North and South. Specifically, the research examines how the Biafra crisis 1) instigated a desire to intervene through humanitarian aid in Denmark, Finland, Norway, and Sweden; 2) gave rise to a new form of large-scale humanitarian aid activities that intensified the interaction between civil society, the media, and the state in the Nordic countries; and 3) influenced post-colonial relations between the North and the global South.

Through an examination of civil society organizations, media discourse, and political dynamics, our goal is to attain a theo-

---

Press, 2021), 171-193; Carl Marklund, "The Moral Diplomacy of Decolonisation: Swedish Responses to the Rising Global South, 1950s-1970s," in *Economia & Lavoro*, Anno LV, 2 (2021), 35–57; Norbert Götz, Georgina Brewis, and Steffen Werther, *Humanitarianism in the Modern World: The Moral Economy of Famine Relief* (Cambridge: Cambridge University Press, 2020); Norbert Götz and Irène Herrmann, "Universalism in Emergency Aid before and after 1970: Ambivalences and Contradictions", *Nationalism and Internationalism Intertwined: A European History of Concepts Beyond the Nation State*, ed. by Pasi Ihalainen and Antero Holmila (New York: Berghahn, 2022), 247–269; Norbert Götz, "Towards Expressive Humanitarianism: The Formative Experience of Biafra", *An Era of Value Change: The Seventies in Europe*, ed. by Fiammetta Balestracci, Christina von Hodenberg, and Isabel Richter (Oxford: Oxford University Press, forthcoming 2024), 207–232.

retically and historically informed comprehension of the pivotal elements influencing Nordic civil society's involvement with and stance toward global humanitarian crises, transcending the confines of the Biafran context. Consequently, our project not only prompts ethical inquiries into humanitarian endeavours, relevant for subsequent studies on global aid, but also fosters a more profound investigation into the broader Nordic role in civil society engagement within international humanitarian cooperation. The ongoing crises in Gaza and other global regions emphasize the critical importance of a well-founded understanding of both the potential and constraints inherent in humanitarian action.

To establish important facts and critical perspectives on the complex post-colonial conflict and subsequent humanitarian aid effort, the BIAFRA project convened a witness seminar at Södertörn University on 18 October 2023. Four Nordic journalists who reported from the Nigerian Civil War – Uno Grönkvist (Sweden), Lasse Jensen (Denmark), Pierre Mens (Sweden), and Pekka Peltola (Finland) – engaged in discussions about their respective Biafra experiences in conversation with researchers Susan Lindholm and Carl Marklund. The following text is based on a transcript of the conversations from that day, which has been edited for improved readability and clarity.

Carl Marklund & Norbert Götz

Participants

Witnesses

Uno Grönkvist (b. 1934), Swedish journalist, communications officer and author. During the Biafra crisis he was a member of the steering group and chief of the communication department of the Swedish Red Cross.

Lasse Jensen (b. 1946), Danish foreign correspondent and news executive for Danish radio and TV channels who worked in Biafra first as a reporter and then as an information officer for the World Council of Churches. In 2000–2001 he made and produced the film *Jesus Christ Airlines* on the Biafran airlift.

Pierre Mens (b. 1939), Swedish photojournalist who has worked for Rädda Barnen, the Swedish Save the Children, and collaborated with Carl Gustaf von Rosen in conjunction with the latter's support activities in Biafra.

Pekka Peltola (b. 1941), Finnish political scientist and journalist, counsellor to the Finnish Ministry of Labour and expert for the Nordic Africa Institute. During the Biafra crisis he worked with filmmaking for Finnish public TV on the crisis and on the humanitarian aid effort.

Interviewers and active seminar participants

Gloria Chuku, Professor, University of Maryland
Norbert Götz, Professor, Södertörn University
Martin Johansson, Researcher, Södertörn University
Susan Lindholm, Senior Lecturer, Stockholm University
Carl Marklund, Associate Professor, Södertörn University
William Sharman, Independent Researcher

Abbreviations

BBC	British Broadcasting Corporation
EU	European Union
ICRC	International Committee of the Red Cross
INALWA	International Airlift West Africa (Red Cross)
JCA	Joint Church Aid
MFI	Malmö Flygindustri (Swedish aviation company)
NATO	North Atlantic Treaty Organization
OAU	Organization of African Unity
RAF	Royal Air Force
SAS	Scandinavian Airlines System
SVT	Sveriges Television AB (Swedish Television Stock Company)
UN	United Nations
USAF	US Air Force
WCC	World Council of Churches
Yle	Yleisradio Oy (The Finnish Broadcasting Company)

Fig. 1–2: The witness seminar at Södertörn University, 18 October 2023: Pekka Peltola, Uno Grönkvist, Lasse Jensen, Pierre Mens, as well as interviewers Susan Lindholm and Carl Marklund (Photo: Norbert Götz).

Witness Seminar part 1

Norbert Götz

Warmly welcome to this witness seminar on Nordic media and the Biafra crisis. Allow me to provide a brief orientation to this afternoon, covering the format of the seminar, our chosen topic, and introducing our esteemed guests. The witness seminar is an oral history method where interviewers engage with a select group of individuals who have experienced a specific historical moment. This method of collective historical reconstruction was originally developed by the Institute of British Contemporary History. In Sweden it has found prominence through the Institute of Contemporary History at Södertörn University. We record our witness seminars and subsequently publish them in the series *Samtidshistoriska frågor*, or *Issues of Contemporary History*. A witness seminar does not aim to establish a singular truth – that is why several voices are being represented. Rather, it is stimulating a variety of perspectives that illustrate how different people involved make sense of the past in their unique ways.

Now, as a background to the narratives that we are going to hear during this seminar, let me provide a concise overview of the Biafra crisis. I hope my outline, while attempting to remain noncontroversial, acknowledges the inherent debate and controversy that is inherent in the writing of history.

Nigeria, a colonial creation, gained independence in 1960. Already after a few years, one of the major ethnic groups, the Igbo people, were exposed to atrocities and massacres. In May 1967, the eastern province of Nigeria, predominantly inhabited by the Igbo, declared independence under the name Republic of Biafra. By July, the Federal Military Government of Nigeria went to war to reclaim the secessionist province. This conflict remained a civil war in Africa, distinct from the UN and Cold War dynamics. Parallel to their military effort, the Nigerians imposed an economic blockade on Biafra. As the area was densely populated and traditionally relied on food imports, a famine began to emerge. The situation was aggravated by Nigerian military progress that turned Biafra into an enclave within Nigeria, and at the same time made millions of Igbos flee to the shrinking territory of Biafra. Many refugees fled because of their fear of genocide. By June 1968, devastating reports and images from Biafra began to circulate that shook the world. Biafra became the first televised famine and a platform for a new, more direct form of photojournalism.

Until this point in time, Red Cross and church aid had been limited, but now an urge to collect money and provide food emerged. Supplies were sent and started to pile up on two islands off the Nigerian coast, the then still Spanish Fernando Po,[2] with the International Committee of the Red Cross (ICRC), and São Tomé, a Portuguese colony that was the base for the World Council of Churches (WCC) and Caritas. By August, the Swedish aviator Carl Gustaf von Rosen[3] broke the Nigerian blockade and established an air link to Biafra. The bush road in Biafra that was turned into a makeshift airstrip became, so the story goes, the second busiest airport in Africa after Johannesburg. Von Rosen himself was briefly Chief of Operations of Nordchurchaid, a joint body of Nordic church aid organizations, such as Lutherhjälpen in Sweden. Nordchurchaid operated the airlift on behalf of church aid organizations from two dozen countries. Joint Church Aid

---

[2] The island was then known in English as Fernando Po (Portuguese: Fernando Pó; Spanish: Fernando Poo). The current name, Bioko, dates from 1979 and is in honour of Equatoguinean soldier and politician Cristino Seriche Bioko. Bioko's native name is *Ëtulá a Ëri* in the Bube language.

[3] Count Carl Gustaf Ericsson von Rosen (1909–1977) was a Swedish pioneer aviator, humanitarian, and mercenary pilot. He flew relief missions in a number of conflicts as well as combat missions for Finland (whose first military aircraft his father had donated in 1918) and Biafra. His flights for the Biafran Air Force were notable for using the small Malmö MFI-9 in a ground attack role (see below).

(JCA) was the name of this wider group, an exemplary collaboration of Protestant and Catholic churches.

However, controversies arose as von Rosen blurred the lines between humanitarian aid and military support, leading to his resignation. He later smuggled small Swedish training aircraft into Biafra, equipped them with missiles and bombs and flew devastating raids against Nigerian targets together with Swedish and Biafran pilots. The Nigerian response – at least some believe it was a response – was shooting down a Swedish Red Cross airplane. This led to the end of the global Red Cross airlift in June 1969.

By contrast, the churches resumed and amplified the airlift even further. At this point in time, the Biafran situation began to deteriorate rapidly, and in January 1970 the secessionists surrendered. In all, more than 2,000 Red Cross flights and more than 5,000 flights by Joint Church Aid added up to the second largest airlift in history until our time. Only the Berlin Airlift of 1948/49, when the US government was eager to contain Soviet Cold War expansion, was larger. However, while the achievement of the Biafran airlift with respect to humanitarian deliveries is undisputed, its wider consequences are not uncontroversial. Although having fed millions, the airlift has faced criticism for inadvertently prolonging the civil war for almost one and a half years. It is thus said to unnecessarily have prolonged the same humanitarian crisis that it tried to resolve.

Be this as it may, media played a crucial role for mobilizing solidarity for Biafra. Today we are honoured to bring together four distinguished journalists from three Nordic countries who will share their personal experiences of the Biafran War and the humanitarian efforts launched to help the affected population more than fifty years ago. Allow me to briefly introduce our esteemed panellists whose collective insights promise to provide a rich and multifaceted perspective on this critical historical period. Over the years, all our witnesses have received prestigious journalistic prizes, but I will not go further into any details like this.

I start here with this gentleman, Lasse Jensen, the junior of our interviewees, 76 years old. He has been a foreign correspondent and news executive for Danish radio and TV channels and for the past 20 years has worked as a media commentator and analyst. In May 1969 he spent ten days inside Biafra as a reporter and in the second half of 1969 five months as an information officer for the World Council of Churches. He came back to Nigeria, Biafra, and São Tomé in 2000–2001 for making the film *Jesus Christ Airlines* on the Biafran airlift.[4] The name "Jesus Christ Airlines" is known as an alternative interpretation of the acronym JCA, which conventionally stands for Joint Church Aid, but which was uplifted or given a second meaning by being taken for "Jesus Christ Airlines."

Next to him we have Pierre Mens, born in 1939, thus 84 years old. He is a Swedish photojournalist who has worked in ninety countries and been involved in more than twenty books. First, he visited São Tomé and Biafra for a week, working for *Rädda Barnen*, the Swedish branch of Save the Children, and later he followed Carl Gustaf von Rosen on his arms smuggling and air war excursion into Biafra.

Here, closer to me, we have Pekka Peltola, born in 1941, 82 years old. He has a PhD in political science and worked as a journalist, counsellor to the Finnish Ministry of Labour and an expert for the Nordic Africa Institute. He has worked on Namibia and South Africa and written a book on Finland and national liberation in South Africa. He was in Biafra for three days in the critical phase of the establishment of the airlift in August 1968 making a film for Yle, the Finnish Broadcasting Company.[5] On this occasion, he also stayed two weeks on São Tomé. Two more trips to São Tomé in September 1968 followed.

And finally, we have Uno Grönkvist, the senior in this circle, 89 years old. He has a background as a journalist, communications officer, and author. During the Biafra crisis he was a member of the steering group and chief of the communication department of the Swedish Red Cross. In connection with the establishment of the Red Cross airlink in September 1968, he visited Biafra

---

[4] *Jesus Christ Airlines* (2001).

[5] *Biafra: Kuvia afrikkalaisesta sodasta* (1968), YLE archives.

for one day and stayed two weeks on the island of Fernando Po, which was the base of the International Committee of the Red Cross.

Warmly welcome! I think our witnesses who have come here to inform us deserve an applause already at this point. *[Applause.]* And with this, I pass the floor to my colleagues.

Susan Lindholm

Thank you, Norbert, for providing us with an insightful introduction to this complex historical event, which surprisingly feels quite recent when we consider the ongoing media coverage of crises. Today, our aim is to illuminate the Biafra crisis through this witness seminar. In the first part of our session, we will delve into the connection between Biafra and media experiences. We have asked our esteemed panellists to kick the discussion off with a brief five-minute introductory statement. To keep things organized, I suggest we follow the seating order. Pierre, if you wouldn't mind starting us off, please?

Pierre Mens

Alright, thank you. To provide a proper context, I believe it is essential to share some of my background before I travelled into Biafra. In 1961, I was in Ethiopia for three months to produce a photo book, *Haile Selassies land*, featureing a foreword by Prince Bertil.[6] During my travels across the country, I witnessed conditions such as elephantiasis, leprosy, undernourishment among the impoverished, and instances of sudden death. There I also became acquainted with Carl Gustaf von Rosen. In 1962, I went to Tanganyika to make another photo book, this time with a preface by Swedish Prime Minster Tage Erlander.[7] These trips made me get in touch with *Rädda Barnen*, Lutherhjälpen and Radiohjälpen and resulted in TV-films about leprosy in the Lake Victoria region and in Ethiopia, as well as TBC and cholera epidemics in Yemen.[8] By

[6] Allan Hofgren (ed.), *Haile Selassies land: Ett bildverk om svenskarnas insatser i Etiopien* (Stockholm: Ev. fosterl.-stift., 1961).

[7] Allan Hofgren (ed.), *Tanganyika: Ett bildverk om svenska insatser i Afrika* (Stockholm: Filadelfia, 1963).

[8] *8 av 10: En film om människor i det glömda landet* (1964); *Vita pesten* (1965).

the time I went to Biafra on 16 August 1968, I was well-versed in the challenges faced by various African regions.

It was a dramatically eventful departure aboard a Transair DC-7 named "Borås" from Bulltofta Airport in Malmö.[9] Just as we were about to leave, we received an alarming message from the tower: "The plane is under a bomb-threat. Return immediately and evacuate." Fortunately, it turned out to be a false alarm. On the way down to Biafra, we loaded aid from Caritas in Frankfurt. After a refueling stop in the Canary Islands, we finally arrived at São Tomé at lunchtime the following day.

"The first thing that dies is the truth", is an old cliché about war. But I had read about Nigeria and about Biafra's secessionist regime under the leadership of Ojukwu.[10] After independence in 1960, a series of military coups had taken place and Yakubu Gowon had appointed himself as leader of Nigeria.[11] However, he was not accepted by the military governor of the Eastern Region, Ojukwu, who belonged to the Igbo tribe. Among other ethnic groups suspicions grew of all Igbos, who were subjected to persecution, and 30,000 Igbos were brutally murdered. Igbos now fled from the whole country to Biafra, which became overpopulated.

The Gowon regime, with significant help from England's Canberra bombers and Russia's MiG fighter jets and Ilyushin bombers, engaged in relentless warfare. Pilots from East Germany,

---

[9] Transair Sweden AB was a Swedish charter airline that operated until 1981. From 1965 nine Douglas DC-7B were bought from Eastern Airlines and were added to the fleet for charter use and for flights during the civil war in Congo on behalf of the United Nations. Freight flights on behalf of SAS were begun to cities such as Malmö, Copenhagen, Hamburg, Amsterdam, and Paris. Shortly thereafter SAS took a majority holding in Transair Sweden and the airline was kept flying independently under its own colours taking tourists to Spain, the Canary Islands, and other Mediterranean destinations.

[10] Chukwuemeka "Emeka" Odumegwu Ojukwu (1933–2011) was a Nigerian military officer and politician who served as leader of the Republic of Biafra from 1967 to 1970 during the Nigerian Civil War.

[11] Yakubu Dan-Yumma "Jack" Gowon (1934–) is a retired Nigerian army general and military leader. As head of state of Nigeria 1966–1975, Gowon led the country during the Biafra crisis and held the famous "no victor, no vanquished" speech at the war's end to promote reconciliation.

Egypt, and South Africa flew these aircraft, mercilessly targeting schools, markets, and hospitals. The Federal Military Government of Nigeria had also decided to prevent all airplanes from landing in Biafra, obstructing the flow of essential provisions. This cynical hunger blockade affected especially children and the elderly, depriving them of access to food. Many believed that Lagos was ruled by a coup *junta*. Ojukwu belonged to the constitutional government that the Junta overthrew and partly murdered. This was a media picture of the situation in Nigeria, as seen from New York – with the outstanding *New York Times* reporter Garrison[12] – and from London, Berlin, and Sweden.

After a few hours of rest on São Tomé, we started our approach to Biafra. It was a late afternoon and Captain Bengt Lindwall flew at an extremely low altitude. When we crossed the Niger Delta after about two hours, the altitude was 30 to 40 meters. When we landed at Uli, it was almost dark. The airfield was a widened stretch of a straight country road that for night flights was lit up by car headlights and oil lamps made of old tin cans. The call sign was "Annabelle."

I got to sleep over at a Catholic priest's place, and the next morning I drove off with my rental car and a guide to Aba.[13] After a few dozen miles we stopped at a mission station. There I got my life's shock. Lots of children lay unconscious, dried out with swollen bellies. I hid behind my film camera and did my job. Outside, wrapped in rags, lay many dead. The staff said they were without anything – water, medicine, or food. When I was done, I walked around the corner and threw up. We continued towards Aba. The roads were filled with refugees who flocked into Biafra with their belongings. Children carried children on their backs, wheelbarrows, bikes, and cars were overloaded. Upon reaching Aba, the city appeared nearly deserted. At the station there was a crowded train waiting to leave. The gasoline price was 60 kronor

---

[12] Daniel E.Slotnik, "Lloyd Garrison, 83, Journalist; Covered Africa for The Times," *New York Times*, 1 July 2014.

[13] Aba was among the larger settlements of Biafra.

per litre,[14] and the only food available was grilled mountain rats and palm wine to drink.

On the way back to the Uli airfield there were many who sought a ride with us. Once there, I was waiting for the plane to come. At the break of night, Bengt Lindwall landed the DC-7. Quick unloading, and then we started towards São Tomé again, flying at treetop height. We saw muzzle flames on the ground, but we were not hit. We landed at midnight and exhaustion was compact.

After spending a couple of days in São Tomé I managed to get a seat on one of arms dealer Hank Wharton's planes up to Lisbon. From there I made my way back to Stockholm, where *Rädda Barnen* organized a press conference. My photos were shown and circulated, and my film was sent directly to Swedish TV for cutting and editing.[15] Working for an aid organization, it is crucial that the details one provides are a hundred percent correct. I could neither vouch for the number of deaths at the mission station or the number of refugees on the road, just that there were many, many. At the press conference that I attended were roughly two dozen newspapers and radio- and TV-channels.

Susan Lindholm

Thank you so much for this sketch, which is both historical and personal. Next is Lasse – please.

Lasse Jensen

Thanks for the kind introduction. It is very difficult to be brief about my Biafra experience. Not only did Biafra kickstart my journalistic career – the war and the Biafran airlift almost ended my life when I after two years of endless research and fundraising produced and directed a documentary film about Joint Church Aid – JCA – known as "Jesus Christ Airlines". The film project almost drove me into bankruptcy in 2001, and it brought me into

[14] About 11 to 12 USD at the time.

[15] The film was about Save the Children's fundraising work and administration, including street interviews with donors and film clips from the aid work in the Middle East and Nigeria-Biafra. *Skramla för liv* (1968).

hospital with a massive heart attack. But that was more than twenty years ago, and as you can see, I am still alive.

For almost half a century, the Biafra story kept coming back to me. Not as nightmares or other symptoms of post-traumatic stress, but as a continuing journalistic and personal urge. All the time during the past half-century, I realized that there were more stories hidden inside the story, and I welcome the opportunity here to talk about one aspect of a fascinating tale: that of the media and Biafra.

Let me take you back to February 1969. Richard M. Nixon had been president of the United States for less than two weeks when his national security advisor, Henry Kissinger, who, by the way, celebrated his 100th birthday the other day, gave him a briefing about the civil war in Nigeria. The federal government, Kissinger wrote to Nixon, conducted, quote, "the war with often incredible ineptness both in battle and public relations".[16] As for the Biafrans, Kissinger admired their fight against weighty odds and described, quote, "their cynical public relations use of the starvation".[17]

In that context, I was a 22-year-old green, newly trained journalist. I was probably a cog in the wheel. I went to Biafra as a reporter for the Danish news agency, invited by the churches. And when I came home after ten days inside, Pastor Viggo Mollerup,[18] who was the dynamic secretary general of DanChurchAid and one of the masterminds and heads of the Protestant–Catholic airlift, persuaded me to take a job inside Biafra as an information officer for the World Council of Churches. I took the job and spent almost half a year inside Biafra, the first and only time in my

---

16 Memorandum: The White House, Washington, Tuesday, January 28, 1969, Memorandum for the President from: Henry A. Kissinger, subject: U. S. Options in Biafra Relief, Foreign Relations, 1969–1976, Volume E-5, Documents on Africa, 1969–1972, available at https://2001-2009.state.gov/r/pa/ho/frus/nixon/e5/55258.htm (accessed 7 Feb. 2024).

17 Ibid.

18 Viggo Mollerup (1930–2006), Danish priest and aid official, M.Sc. from Copenhagen University 1959, vocation chaplain at Absalon Church in Copenhagen (1960–1964), from where he joined DanChurchAid as secretary, later general secretary (1966–1976). During the years 1976–1990 Viggo Mollerup worked as a parish priest in Vedbæk.

life that I "crossed" the line between independent journalism and public relations. I wrote weekly press releases, met visiting journalists at Uli Airport night after night, and took them around Biafra. I spent considerable time contacting and establishing relations with Biafran officials, who for the most part were Catholics and regarded the Protestant World Council of Churches as merely a subdivision of the influential Catholic Caritas International's relief operation.

Why did I join the WCC in Biafra? In hindsight, I now realize that my motives back in 1969 were more selfish than altruistic. I was adventurous and ambitious, and as one of the relief pilots, Phil Phillp, many years later told me when I reminded him that they had made very good money flying into Biafra, he said. "Well, helping starving children is a good cause, isn't it?"

Shortly after the war ended, Danish journalist Lars Møller-Rasmussen published a book titled *Presse og magt* (The Press and Power) where he used me as an example of the young, inexperienced journalists whom the churches targeted and coveted and invited on press tours to Biafra.[19] And in my case: recruited to do their PR work to raise awareness and money for the relief operation.

Twenty years later, I worked in the same newsroom as the author of those lines, and we became friends. Of course, we discussed his old book and his criticism of my Biafra experience, many hours of it. At one stage, he almost admitted that I was not to blame, and I almost admitted that he had a point in that I was also used as a journalist, for a good cause. The fundraising and awareness work of the churches was incredibly effective. In that context, we realized that – one way or another – the Biafran experience had a huge impact on both our personal and journalistic lives.

My time is almost up, I know, and I could talk for hours about Biafra. It was a disaster in the shadow of Vietnam – the first televised war, and I spent a year in Vietnam as a correspondent. However, Biafra became the first televised famine and the pictures

---

[19] Lars Møller-Rasmussen, *Presse og magt: Manipulation og fordrejning i mediernes nyhedsdækning* (Copenhagen: Gyldendal, 1972), 52.

of starving children in Africa had a huge effect. Today, we have more or less become immune to such images due to what some call "disaster fatigue". Hunger, war, and devastation today produce a never-ending tapestry of horrors. When judging the so-called media war surrounding the civil war in Nigeria., it is crucial to consider the state of the media at that time. Television was powerful, still-pictures were immensely powerful, the perceived threat of "genocide" was powerful at a time when most people still remembered the Second World War and the Holocaust. And in the 1960s, Africa held a significant presence in the media, a prominence that has now dwindled. The so-called media landscape has, by the way, undergone a profound transformation from mass media to a mass of different medias. I look very much forward to the continued hearing. Thank you.

Susan Lindholm

Thank you very much. We will certainly revisit these fascinating points you have raised after the round of introductory statements. Now, Uno, the floor is yours, please.

Uno Grönkvist

Like Pierre, I initially prepared my statement in Swedish, but Carl convinced me to present it in English instead. This will supposedly make it easier for you. I am not sure that is the way it will turn out, but we will see how it goes. – Actually, this is a bizarre situation, isn't it? Here we are, four old men, still alive, trying to remember events in West Africa more than fifty years ago. Quite a memory challenge, isn't it? At the same time, there are currently two other wars going on in the spotlight of world media, and it is essential to keep that in mind. As I have only five minutes like my friends here, I am going to read my statement to ensure a more efficient delivery compared to speaking without notes.

So why was I involved in the Biafra War? One obvious reason was the media coverage. I was, like everyone else, touched by the pictures showing starving children in Biafra. One obvious reason, and that was even more important, was that I had no choice. It was my duty to get engaged. At that time, I was employed by the Swedish Red Cross as head of information and fundraising. I was in charge of all media contacts, but my most important task was to raise money for this large-scale relief operation. With such a focus, I did not have much time to go abroad. Mainly, I followed the war from a Swedish observation point. Even so, I believe I can claim that I was better updated than most of the reporters in the field, as I was involved in the decision-making and had access to confidential information.

Just to give you a background, a few words about the Red Cross. It is the world's largest humanitarian network, represented in 190 countries. We had, at the time of the Biafra War, almost half a million individual members in Sweden. It goes without saying that internal information was very important. I was the publisher of the Red Cross news magazine, distributed to all members. The Swedish Red Cross took a leading role from the very beginning. We bought half a dozen aircrafts, mainly Douglas DC-6 and DC-7, and employed pilots from Sweden and many other countries around the world. This was a unique action, sparking a surge in media interest. Journalists were actively covering the developments right from the onset. Biafra, intertwined with the Red Cross, became a matter of concern for the whole Swedish population at the time.

However, I visited Biafra, of course, first spending several days, as you heard in the introduction, on the island of Fernando Po, then a Spanish colony used as a base for the Red Cross. I made interviews, shot photographs, and took part in the preparation of establishing what is called The International Air Lift West Africa (in short, INALWA).

Finally, I went to Biafra twenty-four hours before the airlift was launched. It was a night flight in complete darkness. The leader of federal Nigeria, General Gowon, had announced that the Red Cross aircrafts should be shot down and flying in the daytime was no alternative.

I will never forget the following day in Biafra! There was no airfield, only a paved road, no landing lights, no nothing. If time permits later, I am prepared to explain how it became possible to use this road as an airstrip. I was afraid, everyone was. We all knew that the base could be attacked. That did not happen, thanks God, not that day, but later, when the airlift was in full swing it did happen.

Finally, what did the Biafra experience mean for my personal development? This was a war in which hunger was used as a weapon! I will never forget the starving children I met. Several of them died in front of my eyes. I was impressed by the work carried through by the many relief workers who risked their lives, every day. Professionally, I gained experience that was of great use when, a few years later, I worked as a Red Cross delegate in civil wars in Uganda and the Middle East. Thank you for listening.

Susan Lindholm

Thank you, Uno, for sharing your experience, and now, Pekka, it is your turn to give us the concluding introductory presentation.

Pekka Peltola

Thank you. My engagement with Biafra had a dual background. I was sitting on two chairs, in fact. Two years before the war I had been selected to the first news department of the Finnish Broadcasting Company. My responsibility there was to oversee the foreign news desk. At the same time, I was editor-in-chief of a magazine, which is still published today, called *Ydin*, a publication associated with the peace movement. Having written about Biafra early on, I had a stand in favour of independent Biafra. And I was aware of the potential conflict of interest. Therefore, when I was working as a journalist, I tried to be as balanced as possible, considering that I was in favour of Biafran independence. It was very natural for me as a Finn to think like that, because of our own history.

So, suddenly I got a call from the news chief – "Pekka, would you be willing to go to Biafra tomorrow at 6 p.m.? You will be provided with a thousand dollars in cash, a cameraman, and a ticket to Lisbon. Try to find your way." They had heard that there were flights going from Lisbon to Biafra. And so, without consideration for malaria, yellow fever and so on, we just embarked on this journey. It took about a week in Lisbon to figure out a way to reach Biafra. There was a firm called Markpress[20] in Switzerland that helped us to find a gun runner called Hank Wharton,[21] known to fly occasionally from Lisbon. We eventually boarded his plane, not entirely sure where we were going now. We went at night, and then we landed in Guinea-Bissau, and went over the runway. The plane was damaged to a minor extent, and only after three days were we able to continue to São Tomé.

And from São Tomé we just worked our way to the next flight to Biafra. We boarded the plane together with Danish and Dutch journalists. It was a difficult flight, and when we started going downward, we were shot at all the time. When we already saw the lights of the runway, the word came that the runway had been bombed and we could not land, and that we must return to São Tomé – two hours, two and a half hours flight. And so, we, me and the cameraman I had with me, we decided to go home now, especially because when we came to São Tomé on 22 August, we heard in the taxi that tanks had entered Prague. The news suggested that nobody would be interested in a small country like Biafra anymore, and perhaps it was time for us to return home. However, we chose not to go home, even after the initial unsuccessful flight, and on the next day we boarded another one. This time we successfully landed at Uli and then proceeded to the front line.

At that time, it was possible for journalists to go to the front, conduct interviews and engage with the people there. It was much freer than it is nowadays, even in places like Ukraine. As a result, we could witness firsthand aspects such as the hunger situation. We could see that hunger prevailed in refugee camps, but not in the streets, as there was no rationing of food or anything like that.

---

[20] The Biafran leadership commissioned a Geneva-based PR agency called Markpress, which served as Biafra's public diplomacy arm for the duration of the war.

[21] "Daring Airlift Director; Henry Arthur Warton," *New York Times*, 30 July 1968.

People could buy food on the streets anywhere, although the food was expensive. Cigarettes were extremely expensive and, of course, any alcoholic beverages.

So, navigating between these two somewhat conflicting roles of a Biafra sympathizer and a journalist, I undertook my work. In connection with the current seminar, I was able to retrieve the documentary film from Biafra that I made together with my cameraman in the Yle-archives. At the time intended for the Finnish public, I have now shared it with the seminar organizers, and I am actually quite proud of it. I managed to somewhat veil my sympathies, at least to a certain extent. *[Laughter.]* But of course, I did not go to the federal side of the conflict, so the film retained a one-sided perspective in that regard. However, when I later came to São Tomé, I made a film on the island, which, at the time, was still a colony under the dictatorship of Salazar in Portugal.

Susan Lindholm

Could you come to a close? Five minutes pass by swiftly.

Pekka Peltola

Aha, okay! But this background is crucial. So, I worked for the Finnish Broadcasting Company and at the same time for this paper, alongside contributing to other papers, and upon my return I went around for speaking engagements and discussions. Our experiences garnered a lot of interest in Finland, and I was invited to speak at numerous events, something for which I got the approval of my boss. I was paid so much for this that I was able to pay back all my study debts – not only mine, but also my wife's. In this way, I benefitted significantly from Biafran hunger, although my primary motivation was, of course, the severe starvation we witnessed in Biafra. We saw it in the camps, where children were dying before our eyes. We actually filmed it, but the footage could not be aired.

Lastly, what did Biafra mean? It was of fundamental importance for my work, for my job, for my professional career. It was this to such a degree that, after the Biafra crisis was over, I went to a publishing company and started making books, my own included. I have not done so much journalistic work since, except when I was in Angola, there I made a couple of documentaries. Thank you.

Susan Lindholm
Thank you so much. Collectively, the four of you have opened numerous avenues and delved into many issues that we are eager to explore further. Particularly noteworthy, Lasse, is your observation that the media landscape was completely different at the time of the Biafra crisis. It is crucial to understand that in the beginning of the 1960s most people did not have TVs in their homes, but that by the end of the decade TVs in private homes were widespread, and that the images from Biafra really entered people's homes. Thus, the Biafra War was really a media war, or a televised war for the first time in history. We also need to remember that a lot of other things happened in 1968, an iconic year that brought significant societal shifts. However, before we delve into that, I would like to explore in more detail how and why each of you got involved in Biafra. Perhaps we start with you, Lasse, because you were there for the longest time. So, the year is 1969, it is May, you are 22 years old, and you find yourself in an interview with Viggo Mollerup, who tells you: "join me and come to Biafra."

Lasse Jensen
No, it was actually after I finished my journalistic training at a local newspaper. I landed, you know, the most wonderful job. First of all, I was allowed to come to Copenhagen from a small provincial town – that was a big thing for me in itself. And I got a position at the Danish National News Agency, Ritzau. As part of that job, I was interviewing Viggo Mollerup, the head of Danish Church Aid. He was also one of the key figures in the Biafran airlift, along with Father Tony Byrne, the Catholic priest. They worked both together and against each other. We can come to that later, there are many fascinating stories about that. Viggo Molle-

rup, after I had interviewed him, straight forwardly asked me, “Oh, we are organizing a tour to Biafra for journalists, would you like to join? There will be four journalists, would you like to come?” And I eagerly rushed back to my editor and asked, “I have been invited to a press tour to Biafra, can I go?” “Yes”, the editor said, “go”.

Two days later, I was on a plane bound for Biafra. That was my first foreign assignment. It was also my first long flight in a DC-6 that smelled of stockfish, all the way down through Africa, carefully avoiding Nigerian airspace. We landed at São Tomé before boarding another plane to Biafra. I was there for only ten days, but those ten days in May 1969 were very crucial because there were two major news stories.

One of the stories concerned the capture of a group of Italian oil engineers by the Biafrans and what I found out – actually what I was told by the head of the Biafran Bureau for External Publicity, who was the very well-known poet and author Cyprian Ekwensi. He told me, sort of took me aside and said, “by the way, we have sentenced them to death, these Italian engineers”. My immediate reaction was, this is a big, big story. And I then sent a telegram back. At that time there was one Telex link from Biafra that went through Lisbon and to Markpress in Geneva (that is another story because Markpress was the official Biafran public relations agency). But I was not allowed to mention the death sentence, I had to write in English – it was a war, there was censorship. However, I said, I have to add a few lines of technical information in Danish, and they said, okay. And then I added the two lines which read, replace introduction with the following: “Biafran sources, authoritative sources, tell me they have been sentenced to death.” With this I suddenly became world famous, not as Lasse Jensen, but as big frontpage news in Italian newspapers, as the Danish journalist “Ritzau”, which was actually the name of the news agency I worked for. *[Laughter.]*

And then, a few days later, the second news story was, of course *[turns to Pierre Mens]*, that your friend von Rosen started his bombing of Nigerian targets with his small planes from Malmö.

And that was also a story of mine – you had the photographic scoop; I had the written scoop.

Pierre Mens
Yes, exactly.

Lasse Jensen
When I came home, I was of course the big man at the news agency. I was the youngest staffer, but I provided Ritzau with two world scoops, which was … of course, I mean, I was then really on top of the world. And then … sorry, Pekka?

Pekka Peltola
You know, I was just about to ask, what were the biggest problems along the way? I would say, especially during my first trip, it was that every day was full of big problems. Sometimes we were shot at, they really aimed at us, and sometimes there was no food and nothing to drink, especially no alcohol, which we would have needed.

Let me give you an example from the second flight. We were on a DC-3, and we were only a handful of journalists, maybe three or four of us. So, I noticed that it was unusually cold and wondered from where the cold air was coming. I went to the back of the plane and found a door slightly open, so I closed it and we continued. It was kind of normal that things would not work as they usually do.

Another example involved theft and a bizarre return. We were robbed, all our camera equipment vanished in Lisbon. However, Hank Wharton, the gun-runner I mentioned earlier, somehow knew where we should try to find our gear. He directed us in a jeep around the airport, and indeed, under one plane, which was not intended for us, we discovered all our belongings in open air, neatly placed in the grass. So, we just collected our stuff, 120 kilos of equipment, and took it with us. And that was it.

Combine such challenges with the constant struggle to find moments of sleep – we slept whenever we could, especially during flights. When we got back to Europe, I remember waking up when something hit my eye. I think it was irritating my eye. It was the sun rising behind the Alps. For me, that meant, I am almost home, this is home, outside there. So, this was the whole thing and when I finally got home, I went to take a bath. But then my wife came and said, there is a call for you. When I went to the phone, my boss told me, you immediately need to come to the studio, we send with direct transmission now, you will be interviewed, and so on.

And as you say, I was a big, big name after that. Yet, it was surreal, of course, the life of a famous journalist is everything ... a journalist. But then I also discovered the downside of fame. When people start to recognize you on the street, maybe the first half an hour this feels nice, but then later it becomes a real problem. This actually influenced my decision not to continue very long my career as a journalist.

Susan Lindholm

Yes, it seems like Biafra gave rise to a multitude of celebrities – anyone who became involved in it.

Lasse Jensen

As I used to say when I later became head of news for Danish television, we were the best news programme in Denmark on television. We were also the worst news programme on television. *[Laughter.]* We were the only news programme on television. Denmark, Norway, Sweden, and Finland each had a monopoly with just one television station. In contrast to today's landscape of social media and commercial television, that means the impact of what we can call the state broadcast, or the public service broadcast, was immense.

I was just going to finish my little story. When I came back from Biafra, Viggo Mollerup invited me for coffee and asked, "Well, by the way, would you like a job in Biafra?" And hey, why not? Two weeks later, I was on another stockfish stinking plane to São Tomé, eventually making my way into Uli, spending six months within Biafra. And I think I experienced about fifty nights on Uli with bombings occurring. Thank God, they only hit once or twice, as they were very bad at it. The Nigerians used a converted DC-6, DC-4, which we called the Intruder, with a Belgian pilot. Our pilots and I who worked for the airlift and the WCC communicated with him on the radio and said, "Hey, you, stinking drunk Belgian fascist, you can't hit us." And he couldn't, only very, very rarely he did.

But I mean, there was this constant pressure night after night on Uli Airport, which was a converted piece of road, as we already heard, which at that time, in '69, had been equipped with real electrical runway lights. These lights were only switched on one to one-and-a-half minutes before landing. For the pilots, this meant an approach in total darkness using a very primitive radio beacon, and then request lights and when you got lights hopefully that runway would be right in front of you. And then they would go down and land. The runway was pretty long, but it was very narrow. Those nights at Uli I will never forget.

Carl Marklund
I wonder about a detail: when you were there for the second time, were you still associated with Ritzau?

Lasse Jensen
No, but I had an agreement with them that allowed me to write stories for them. But they had to state that this story came from an information officer of the World Council of Churches.

Susan Lindholm
Yes, Pekka, would you like to add something?

Pekka Peltola
I think that in some respect this is what the discussion here should be about: Did we have any impact on anything? We certainly had an impact on public opinion, of course we had. But did our impact extend to decision makers and policies? I can share an example from my experience. During the two or three months of my fame

I was invited to a small gathering with the leader of Finnish foreign policy, President Urho Kekkonen, at his residence. Our group was small, providing an opportunity to delve into discussions of Biafra and various other issues. So, my focus in this meeting was the question, "Mr. President, should we not try to convince the Nordic governments to work together – and together recognize Biafra?" That was my agenda, but it failed to make any impression on the president, the sole authority in deciding Finnish foreign policy. He just remarked that only humanitarian aid was feasible, as anything else would pose numerous problems and would not be advisable at all. Therefore, I can say that we did not wield any influence on Finnish foreign policy, although the public opinion might have been very widely on the side of Biafra.

Carl Marklund

Just a quick follow-up on that. Was it ever commented at the time that you as a state-employed journalist held these pro-Biafra views?

Pekka Peltola

No, there was no questioning of it; it was considered quite natural. Remember that I was also editor-in-chief of this peace-movement paper, which was known as an opinion-driven publication with an intellectually leftist and peace-minded orientation. This paper was widely commented also regarding some other things. For example, there were problems with the Finnish–Israeli connection and this was even … this could not even be discussed. The connection was there and is there.

Carl Marklund

Thank you.

Susan Lindholm

That is also the impression I gather listening to you panellists, and when reading about the crisis and media reactions. It seems like you all had multifaceted roles, like functioning both as a journalist and, for example, as a humanitarian aid worker. And, Uno, I would like to bring you into the discussion. You worked for the Red Cross, but you were also a media man. Can you shed light on that? Were you still collaborating with journalists, or did conflicts arise, such as between journalists and photographers? What would you say, from your experience – do you share the experiences of the other panellists?

Uno Grönkvist

Yes, sure. Well, my primary goal, above all else, was to achieve the best possible fundraising outcome in my country, in Sweden. In order to accomplish that, we needed wide publicity, positive publicity about the relief efforts – remaining neutral on the political front. And that means that during this time, because I worked for the Red Cross for the whole period of the Biafran War, I travelled the country *[i.e., Sweden]*. I conducted press conferences, seminars, conferences, met the local papers, regional papers, and of course papers on the national level. The idea was not discussing the war, but rather highlighting what the Red Cross did in order to help the civil population during the conflict.

I would say that the media interest in this war, correct me if I am wrong, was especially high due to the dramatic background of the crisis, namely the plight of the children. Crucial were these pictures of children with their big eyes, the big stomachs, and the very, very thin legs and arms, gazing into the camera, sometimes dying in front of the camera. This stirred reactions in everyone who saw these pictures, and that, I would say, laid the groundwork for very good fundraising results. People could not ignore these children; they could not even sleep because of what these children suffered. A similar situation is observed today in Gaza, of course. So that happens in war after war, but in my opinion, Biafra was the first war where children took centre stage. Lasse, you mentioned Vietnam being the first televised war. I would argue that Biafra was the first televised war on the global level, at least for this part of Europe.

Lasse Jensen
The first televised famine. Well, famine, yes. It was not considered a war; it was seen as a famine. Well, it was the starving children, not the Biafran political situation that interested people, I think.

Uno Grönkvist
Perhaps not, but they are interconnected. There were children in the war, right? And you can see a background in Sweden and the rise of television. Television grew in the 1950s, late 1950s, and early 1960s. The breakthrough for TV in Sweden was in 1958. You know why?

Carl Marklund
The World Cup.

Lasse Jensen
Pardon?

Carl Marklund
The World Cup in football.

Uno Grönkvist
The World Cup, you are right. The World Cup was played in Sweden in 1958.

Lasse Jensen
This was the first time in my life I have watched television.

Uno Grönkvist
The World Cup – there you go. This means there was an outstanding interest in watching these matches. And people, they lined up to buy TVs. After that, you had many TV sets in families across the country, allowing them to watch this war in Biafra. And the television companies, they had the money to send TV teams there – and lots of photographers – Pierre was one of them. Some of the best-known Swedish photographers went to Biafra, like

Björn Larsson Ask, who died a few weeks ago, Anders Engman from Kamerabild, et cetera. They spent a lot of time there, got fantastic pictures. They were accompanied by the best journalists who produced compelling stories. And that carries through all the way to the good results of the fundraising. But as I represent a relief organization, unlike my friends here who represent the media of that time, I can tell you about the beginnings of the Red Cross airlift if you are interested, as it was quite dramatic.

As you heard before, I went to Fernando Po a week before this airlift was established. Sitting in the garden hotel where we had all these crews from different countries, discussions unfolded regarding the initiation of the airlift. To tell you the truth, these pilots were veterans. They had been flying for the United Nations in the Congo, in different parts of the world, in Ethiopia, Abyssinia, et cetera. So, they were no cowards. But in this situation, they were afraid, they were scared, because they had heard the official warnings from Nigeria, if you start flying, we will shoot you down. Everyone knew about it, and it sparked a big discussion. Our leader was Sven Lampell, a Swedish colonel who became the commander of the Red Cross air bridge.[22] I listened to this – I did not take part in the debate, but I listened to it – and it was very exciting, because most of these foreign pilots said, no, we are not prepared to start. We do not want to risk our lives. Then the pilots from Finland said, "*Perkele*,[23] we go. We fly." And when they said that, of course, the pilots from other nations were compelled to follow suit.

---

[22] Sven Lampell (1920–2007) was a Swedish Air Force officer. He was chief of flight operations at Södertörn Wing (F 18) from 1956 to 1960 and chief of staff at the Third Air Command (E 3) in 1960 and was serving with the United Nations in the Congo from 1961 to 1962 and in 1963. Lampell was promoted to colonel in 1965 and wing commander at Hälsinge Wing (F 15). He served in the Swedish Red Cross, involved in the Biafran airlift from 1968 to 1969 and in East Pakistan and Bangladesh from 1971 to 1972. He left the Air Force in 1972 for a position as Chief Delegate at the ICRC in Geneva. The years serving in the Red Cross also involved missions in Jordan, Ethiopia, South Vietnam, Western Sahara, Somalia, and Afghanistan.

[23] *Perkele* is a Finnish word meaning "evil spirit" and a popular Finnish profanity, used similarly to the English phrase "goddamn".

So suddenly, a decision came about. We would start. As mentioned earlier, I entered Biafra twenty-four hours before the airlift started, in the midst of the dark. And I took part in the preparations the following day. There were a lot of issues, as you have heard. There was a road, but no airfield. It was a short, paved road, which was used as the airstrip. But there were no landing lights, nothing. And only a few hours were left before it all was going to begin. So, Sven Lampell sent out local children and teenagers to collect empty bottles in the surrounding villages. They came back with hundreds of bottles and left them to Mr. Lampell, and he and his fellow workers filled these bottles with kerosene, and then inserted cotton waste. These bottles were used as improvised landing lights. They placed them along this road, on both sides, and when the first aircraft arrived at night, they lighted them. It worked, you know, we got perfect landing lights. But the problem was that as soon as the aircraft landed, it blew out all the flames. That means, they had to do it again and again, because when the first plane started for a return to Fernando Po, the next aircraft was waiting to land. So, they had to be there for the whole night, lighting up these bottles, day after day, week after week.

Carl Marklund
May I pose a brief question? You mentioned these foreign pilots, as you call them, gathered on Fernando Po, expressing scepticism about flying. So, did they gather there without knowing that the Nigerians had imposed this kind of air blockade? Didn't they know that when they initially came there? Would they have been expecting to be able to fly into Biafra – is that correct?

Uno Grönkvist
This is a hard question to answer. I guess some of them were aware, while others may not have been, depending on what they were recruited for. But one issue is, what you are thinking at home, the other is, are we prepared to start tomorrow, under per-

sistent threat. And you all know, what happened later on.[24] So, it was dangerous.

Carl Marklund
Just a follow up to that then. We have heard here from Pierre and from Lasse that they went to Biafra, partially also commissioned by aid organizations. How about your role as an information officer of the Red Cross. Did you also commission reporters to come to Biafra to report on the scene?

Uno Grönkvist
Yes, I had various responsibilities. One was to garner as much interest as possible from Swedish mass media, including sending reporters and photographers to Fernando Po and into Biafra, but also to collect information, because we had a variety of different channels through the International Red Cross. So, we got plenty of information we had to assemble, and we had to forward it to different Swedish TV stations, radio, and, of course, newspapers. There was a flow of information, but as we discussed earlier today, some of us, even at that time, even if we lacked the expression for it, realized there was fake news. So, there was the question of what was true and what was fake. That you had to sort out, and that is not an easy task, I would say.

Carl Marklund
It still isn't.

Susan Lindholm
Indeed. Your narrative seems quite similar to Lasse's and echoes his documentary as well – with pilots being recruited internationally without really knowing when and where they would be

---

[24] On the night of 5 June to 6 June 1969, a DC-7B, which had been put at the disposal of the ICRC by the Swedish Red Cross was reported missing. The plane, which was based on Fernando Po, Equatorial Guinea, was on the way to Uli, in Biafra, carrying relief cargo consisting of food. The following inquiry revealed that it was shot down by a Nigerian fighter on 5 June 1969, near Calabar in Eastern Nigeria.

working. What I am curious about is what you are mentioning in the film, Lasse, namely the rivalry, perhaps, between Joint Church Aid and the Red Cross. You were flying from different islands, and you had different landing points. How did you perceive the situation on-site? Because the rivalry might be a narrative constructed afterwards, or what do you think?

Lasse Jensen:
Well, you must understand that when I entered Biafra on behalf of the WCC, I had just come back from my first reporting trip to Biafra when the Swedish Red Cross plane was shot down. I believe I later tracked down the pilot who actually shot it down, but I could never get it confirmed. He was a British MiG pilot. But anyway, when I arrived, the Red Cross had ceased flying due to the shooting down of the Transair plane.[25] So, when I came back, basically, among the pilots the Red Cross was regarded as sissies. The Red Cross, I mean, they didn't have the balls to keep on flying.

We did. We kept on flying despite the Nigerian blockade. Perhaps there was a natural rivalry between us and the well-established Red Cross, which – that is a long story with Dr Lindt and all that[26] – which was trying to navigate internationally between the Federal Military Government, attempting to secure aid for the federal area, and at the same time operating what was in principle an illegal airlift into Biafra.

So, compared with us the Red Cross was in a completely different position. They were in a very, very, very difficult diplomatic political situation between the Biafrans, world opinion, and governments who, for the most part, never recognized Biafra. By

---

[25] The Swedish Red Cross chartered Transair planes for the airlift.

[26] August R. Lindt (1905–2000) was a Swiss lawyer and diplomat, the son of August Ludwig Lindt, a pharmacist and chocolate manufacturer. He served as Chairman of UNICEF from 1953 to 1954 and as United Nations High Commissioner for Refugees from 1956 to 1960. He served as the Ambassador of Switzerland to the United States from 1960 to 1962 and Ambassador to the Soviet Union from 1966 to 1968. He then became General Commissioner of the ICRC for West Africa and later Swiss Ambassador to Mongolia, India, and Nepal. He was an adviser to the President of Rwanda from 1973 to 1975.

contrast, the churches, they were the mavericks. They didn't give a damn. They flew. And, of course, that, among the pilots, created a we-are-the-heroes type of feeling.

The group of pilots was intriguing; I could talk about them for hours. Basically, they represented a generation of pilots who were trained in propeller planes. In those years, in international aviation propeller planes were being replaced by jet airplanes. These pilots, slightly too old for retraining to jets, were looking for jobs. It was very simple. And many of them were, well, I know we have been advised not to delve into too many anecdotes … *[Laughter.]*

One of my favourites when I made my film involved two aging British pilots, an old pilot who used to fly Lancasters and bombed Germany during the Second World War, and his slightly younger co-pilot. They were flying in from São Tomé, passing the Nigerian border, and suddenly Phil *[Phillp]*, the second officer, said, "I think, what is this? What are these explosions in the air? I think we're being shot at by anti-aircraft fire." The captain, who was this old Royal Air Force (RAF) bomber pilot responded, "Don't worry Phil, I've been shot at by experts." *[Laughter.]* And of course, the Nigerians never shot anything down with anti-aircraft fire. Anyhow, there was a rivalry, but when I worked from within Biafra there was no rivalry any longer as the Red Cross had discontinued its flights.

Carl Marklund

I would like to ask, Pierre, about your involvement. You went to Biafra on behalf of *Rädda Barnen* [Save the Children], together with *Rädda Barnen*. The other panellists have been discussing the visuals of the war, and here you have a combination of both the visual and the aerial aspect, so to speak. Could you share a bit about your entry point into Biafra in this context?

Pierre Mens

My first trip was for *Rädda Barnen*, whereas the second was with Carl Gustaf von Rosen.

Carl Marklund

Yes, exactly. And there was no link between them, or am I wrong?

Pierre Mens

The second trip began on 11 May. Von Rosen had tried in every way to get help from politicians including US President Lyndon B. Johnson, U Thant at the United Nations, and Tage Erlander in Stockholm, but nobody showed interest in helping him. Haile Selassie was positive, but he could not rally other African states. On Christmas Day 1968, von Rosen was in Umuahia, then the capital of Biafra, and he presented a letter to Ojukwu from Haile Selassie. That day there were three bombing attacks, one hit a hospital where hundreds of children and adults were killed. After that von Rosen spoke to Fredrick Forsyth,[27] crying "I will come back and crush the Nigerian bomb plane." The idea of using the small "mini-coin" aircraft was born.[28] Carl Gustaf was more African than the Africans. Once he advised Haile Selassie, the best thing Africa could do was going back to bow and arrow, rather than buying bad bombers, weapons from the Soviet Union and East Germany, and instead spend the money on hospitals and education.

Anyhow, the mini-coins were brought to Gabon, where we put the wings on, the pods under the wings, and where we camouflage painted the five aircrafts. Additional fuel tanks were installed on the right seat. We also tested the rockets and trained bush attacks.[29]

---

[27] Fredrick Forsyth b. 1938 is an English novelist and journalist. Forsyth completed his National Service in the RAF as a pilot, joined Reuters in 1961 and in 1965 the BBC, for which he served as an assistant diplomatic correspondent. His earliest media work covered French affairs and reporting on the Nigerian Civil War between Biafra and Nigeria as a BBC correspondent. He later returned to Biafra as a freelance reporter, writing his first book, *The Biafra Story*, in 1969. In 2015 Forsyth revealed that in Biafra he had been an informant for British intelligence, MI6.

[28] The acronym "mini-coin" signifies "miniature counter-insurgency," see also Lasse Jensen's explanation below.

[29] Apart from von Rosen, the pilots were Martin Lang, Gunnar Haglund, Auguste Opke, and Willy Bruce. Mens became part of the mini coins-group

And then, one morning, the planes flew from Gabon to Port Harcourt seeking to damage as many MiG and other bomb planes as possible. The raid was a big success, and the mini-coins even bombed the tower and some magazine for weapons and arms. Although this action was a great success, in the long run conditions became very difficult because the Nigerian bombers from Russia and England were flown by pilots from South Africa, East Germany, and so on. It was too hard to fight against them, so Biafra had to surrender right in the beginning of 1970.

Carl Marklund
Looking at that situation and your role, you were of course collaborating with Carl Gustaf von Rosen, but you had earlier been in Biafra in the capacity of making a film together with *Rädda Barnen*, right?

Pierre Mens
Yes, that is accurate. My initial visit was with *Rädda Barnen* to take pictures and make a film. When I came home, a big press conference took place in Stockholm, attended by numerous newspapers, magazines, radio and television channels. They disseminated my photographs, and my film was sent to the television – there was a lot of interest. When you work for an organization like, say, *Rädda Barnen*, it is crucial to get the facts right, and at that time we did not have any cell phones. I mean, all the figures we had heard in Biafra or at São Tomé – it was very difficult to confidently affirm, this is right, or, this is not right.

Carl Marklund
Does that mean you had to rely heavily on the information that you received in Biafra, so to speak?

---

because von Rosen needed assistance with photographs from the plane during the raids.

Pierre Mens
Ja, absolutely! I mean, one day, they told me "Come to this town, there are a lot of dead people on the street." That was not my own focus, as I rather wanted to talk with the people, observe the situation in the hospitals, look at the mission stations, and so on.

Carl Marklund
In your interaction with the Biafran Information Ministry, did they suggest these locations to you?

Pierre Mens
I didn't have so much contact with them.

Carl Marklund
No, you didn't? So, who guided you and suggested specific locations or topics?

Pierre Mens
I was my own master.

Carl Marklund
You were your own master, okay.

Lasse Jensen
Do I get it right? Your first trip was for *Rädda Barnen*, yes, Save the Children. The second trip was with von Rosen. And the two trips were not connected?

Pierre Mens
No, no, not at all. The only connection was that von Rosen organized my trip for Save the Children.

Carl Marklund
Ah, he did?

Pierre Mens
He was the head pilot of Nordchurchaid at that time.

Carl Marklund
Thank you for clarifying.

Susan Lindholm
It is fascinating that you were able to move around freely. That also concerns a question that I have to you, Lasse, because as an information officer you welcomed journalists who came to Biafra, and they lived with you in that house, and you showed them around. Considering the Markpress agency and all the propaganda efforts surrounding Biafra, the question is: Were you fully free to move around?

Lasse Jensen
Absolutely.

Susan Lindholm
Okay?

Lasse Jensen
No problem.

Susan Lindholm
Well, okay.

Lasse Jensen
I mean, it is because the state of Biafra, which when I was there was a very small state, was landlocked. When a country is at war, we normally … if I was a journalist now, I am not sure that I could just ride freely around Ukraine, or Gaza. There would probably be no way you could do that. But in Biafra there was really no internal security. We were stopped at checkpoints once in a while, but nobody ever asked questions. I had a car with a WCC label and the fishes logo, and we were just waved through unless they wanted

some cigarettes or something we could offer. They always, funnily enough, every European the Igbos saw they called "Father," due to the heavily Catholic area. As a twenty-two-year-old Protestant information officer, I have been called Father more times than ever until I had children of my own. *[Laughter.]* But, no, we could drive around, from north to south, east to west. Biafra, at that time, was perhaps a hundred kilometres that way and maybe a hundred and twenty kilometres north–south. It was a very small, quote-unquote, country, and it was getting smaller and smaller.

Pierre Mens
Day by day.

Lasse Jensen
So, there was no … I mean, when I was there as a journalist, on a trip organized by the churches, we went to Umuahia, which was then the administrative capital, and met, and there was a press conference with Ojukwu, and so on, and so forth. But when we were in the church system, we could drive around freely, and nobody was interested. The only communication channel out was one Telex. There, you had to write in English, as I said. But you could wait to file your stories until you reached São Tomé, where there was no censorship. You could do whatever you wanted.

Carl Marklund
The Portuguese never minded?

Lasse Jensen
No, they didn't care as long as we paid. They were very, very ...

Pierre Mens
Money talks!

Lasse Jensen
And especially in São Tomé.

Carl Marklund
I see.

Susan Lindholm
Uno, I see your hand, but it is 14:20 now, and we are planning to have a break. So maybe, if you could try to remember what you want to say now – or is it just a short comment?

Uno Grönkvist
Very briefly, in response to the earlier question. I think Lasse summed up the situation very well, with one exception. I would say that the Red Cross pilots were just as courageous as those flying for the "Jesus Christ Airline", but it is crucial to acknowledge the difference. The Red Cross possessed a powerful trademark, an excellent image, and a very, very long story and background. Maintaining neutrality was paramount for the organization under all circumstances because it would not function otherwise. Consequently, we had to weigh in a lot of different aspects into our decisions, although this approach might have been perceived by some as somewhat bureaucratic. Indeed, only one year after the end of the war, a new organization emerged, and that was Doctors Without Borders, *Läkare utan gränser.* The founders of this organization believed that the Red Cross was too slow and overly focused on political decisions, et cetera. So, they formed that new organization, which in my opinion is the most effective relief organization existing today, surpassing even the Red Cross, I would say.

Lasse Jensen
Yes, I agree.

Carl Marklund
Thank you so much.

Susan Lindholm
A fitting statement to conclude with, indeed.

Carl Marklund
Thank you. *[Applause.]*

Lasse Jensen
The Red Cross always gets the last word. *[Laughter]*

Carl Marklund
We will now have a half-hour break, and there will be coffee and biscuits available.

Images

Fig. 3. Chairman Erland von Hofsten briefs the Swedish Red Cross steering group for operations in Biafra and the flight crew at Bromma Airport, Stockholm, prior to their departure to Fernando Po and Biafra on 25 August 1968 (Arne Jönsson/DN/TT Nyhetsbyrån).

Fig. 4. Uno Grönkvist, chief of the communication department of the Swedish Red Cross, takes farewell from his fiancee Rita Jörgensen at Bromma Airport, Stockholm, before his departure to Fernando Po and Biafra, 25 Augusti 1968 (Arne Jönsson/DN/TT Nyhetsbyrån).

Fig. 7. JCA staff graveyard at Uli airport, September 1969 (photo courtesy of Lasse Jensen).

Fig. 8. Flight captain Bengt Lindwall in front of the Transair DC-6 "Borås" (photo courtesy of Pierre Mens).

Fig. 9. Father Anthony Byrne looks on as Transair takes off (photo courtesy of Pierre Mens).

Fig. 10. The Red Cross symbol being painted over at São Tomé (photo courtesy of Pierre Mens).

Fig. 11. Refugees in Biafra 1969 (photo courtesy of Pierre Mens).

Fig. 12. Refugees in Aba, Biafra, 1969 (photo courtesy of Pierre Mens).

Fig. 13. Fighters of the Biafran Army in 1969 (photo courtesy of Pierre Mens).

Fig. 14. Painting the mini-coins for camouflage, Carl Gustaf von Rosen to the left (photo courtesy of Pierre Mens).

Fig. 15. One of Carl Gustaf von Rosen's mini-coins making a fly-past (photo courtesy of Pierre Mens).

Fig. 16. Biafrans chatting with Carl Gustaf von Rosen (photo courtesy of Pierre Mens).

Fig. 17. Film poster for *Jesus Christ Airlines*, directed by Lasse Jensen in 2001 (courtesy of Lasse Jensen).

Witness Seminar part 2

Carl Marklund

Thank you very much and warmly welcome back to the second block of this witness seminar we have here today on Biafra and the media. I hope everybody is reenergized by the biscuits offered during the break. We now have a little less than an hour for our next block, which we plan to end around 15:35. Thereafter we will have time for some fifteen minutes of questions from the audience, and then we will provide an opportunity for our witnesses to share their concluding reflections for about three minutes each. We aim to wrap up by 4 o'clock. We have shown here some pictures in the meantime. I do not know how many of you have had a chance to see them, but we are very grateful to our witnesses who shared these visuals.

The set that we are now entering will explore a different aspect than the first one. While we have gained valuable insights from our witnesses into the realities on the ground in Biafra and the circumstances surrounding their visits and activities in Biafra, it is crucial to recognize that Biafra became a significant global media event. As several witnesses have highlighted, the world learned about Biafra primarily through images of starving children, eliciting widespread moral outrage.

Now, shifting the focus in this direction, I would like to address a question. Weren't there any other stories emerging from Biafra? From your position as a journalist, as a witness, could you also see other stories coming out of Biafra, so to speak? Not only about people in refugee camps who were starving, but also stories about resistance, about resilience, about alternative developments? I would like to pose this question first to you, Pekka, because you were on the ground filming for Finnish national television. I wonder what your perspective on this matter is?

Pekka Peltola

Of course, I was trying to connect with, trying to interview people, but inevitably the primary focus shifted to the distressing plight of dying children. Importantly, we encountered them only among refugees from the southern regions, such as the rivers people. In the camps there was almost no food. Although food was coming in, it seemed to be diverted elsewhere, leaving shelves conspicuously bare. Hungry people tend to be very quiet, especially children are almost completely silent.

A challenge arose when we documented severely ill children through photos and film; tragically some died in the film. You cannot show that, that would be too overwhelming for television broadcast. And the emotional toll on us as witnesses was almost unbearable. I always remember, for all my life, the holding of a hand. There was a father holding the hand of a child who was perhaps four years old, and then the son died. The son died while we were filming. It is things like that you cannot forget. A different memory is how the people were walking on the street. They did not openly show that they were hungry, but they sought cigarettes. So, I learned that when a beggar came with the bowl, giving Biafran money was pointless, it held no value. But giving a couple of cigarettes would mean that this person could obtain at least two meals. I had lots of cigarettes from São Tomé, so I could distribute them.

Expanding beyond Biafra, I later covered events in Angola from 1979 to 1987, every year, being present there at least a month. There was also a civil war going on there, but the dynamics were vastly different. Journalists were not allowed to go to the front lines, not even close to them, but we were nevertheless sometimes attacked by military force. It was very different. And then there were ambushes and mines, which we tried to avoid, and of course this conflict lasted much longer than the war in Biafra. It went on and on. One realization in this context is that you get used to fighting. People can fight, especially young people can fight quite easily because they get used to war within a few days. Right after the first attack, they may already have gotten used to it. You cannot feel fear all the time. You just go on. It's not … it's normal.

Carl Marklund
I find your narrative fascinating because it sheds light on the normalcy of the catastrophe, the normalcy of the crisis beyond the desolation experienced by children and mothers in Biafra. I am curious about your efforts and opportunities to convey alternative messages about Biafra and Biafra's resistance. I am thinking, for example, about the fighting forces, the resilience of mothers trying to feed their children, and other different stories. Does this resonate with some of the concerns that you had at the time?

Pekka Peltola
Doing something else?

Carl Marklund
Other than, shall we say, convey the image of the starving child, which is the prevalent global image of Biafra today, what comes to most people's minds when they hear about Biafra. I am interested in whether the panel encountered opportunities to break through with other stories, other narratives. Why did the narrative of the starving child dominate? Amid a civil war and the pursuit of Biafran independence, which many of those on site obviously supported. It is intriguing for us in hindsight to ponder why there was such an immense focus on the suffering of children. Were there no other narratives available?

Pekka Peltola
Well, I am a person who tends to think politically. However, on a different note, while in Biafra and quite often in Angola as well, we possessed some food for personal use, but we could not keep it to ourselves, instead distributing it to those in need. For example, when we were in the mountains [of Angola], we had a school in the mountains, we did not have anything for a week. Not only beer

was out but everything else was too. Although you cannot ultimately help giving your food, if you have seen and felt how bad it is to be hungry, when you see people dying, you just give whatever, anywhere. But then you do not give your last morsel of food unless you know it has some effect. You just think that now my task is writing about this, talking to decision-makers, if possible, and helping those suffering to get needed provisions. The problem that arises then is that they normally ask for weapons, grenades, like in Ukraine today. I do not think this is leading to any kind of solution.

Carl Marklund
Uno, I believe you would like to comment.

Uno Grönkvist
I have a short answer to your question, why focus on the starving children? Because stories about starving children sell newspapers.

Carl Marklund
Is it that cynical?

Uno Grönkvist
It is as simple as that.

Carl Marklund
It was also, of course, the truth. The children were starving.

Uno Grönkvist
It is all about business. I would say, it is all about money.

Susan Lindholm
Lasse, I see that you would like to contribute to the discussion.

Lasse Jensen
Well, when examining the Biafran situation, three dimensions are relevant: the military, the political, and the humanitarian. And in the realm of television, especially television journalism, the critical

question is whether to engage the brain, the gut, or the heart. Every television journalist understands that one may address the brain of the recipient for a short while, but if this becomes too long, the brain will switch off. In contrast, tapping into emotions, addressing the gut, the heart, the audience will stay on.

While this approach might seem cynical, I do not think it is about making cynical decisions, such as "The editor says, we want starving children on the front page because it sells." Rather, this was the story about Biafra because it resonated. Who, excuse me, now fifty-four years later cares a damn whether the Biafran forces advanced a mile and a half in a certain direction, or there is this dimension or that dimension. I think many journalists tried to get the other dimensions into the main narrative.

However, ultimately you end up with stories. How many people think of the Vietnam War today – we talked about it during the break – without remembering the picture of the little girl after a napalm attack. That is probably for many people the memory of Vietnam. Or the execution of a Viet Cong prisoner by the police chief in Saigon because this stirs emotions in the opposite direction, causing disgust. That is the nature of journalism, in a sense – it is to do that.

And basically, the political, the military situation in Biafra was a straightforward narrative. Biafra got smaller and smaller and smaller. The political situation, and we can talk about that at length if we want to, was fundamentally that – although the pictures of the starving children mobilized a lot of sympathy, a lot of money, a lot of this, that, and the other – all this did not have any political effect whatsoever. The Americans, the British, the Scandinavians, the European governments all felt for Biafra, but their foreign policy was, "we support the federal government in Lagos". And that was the way it was because there were overriding foreign policy priorities that took over in that sense.

The way governments grappled with this dilemma, these starving children in the media, was basically by giving a lot of money to the relief organizations. You *[addressing Uno Grönkvist]* and I were trying to raise funds for the Red Cross and the churches, respectively. However, more than 70 per cent of the whole cost of the airlift and the Red Cross airlift, I believe, was funded by governments. It was government money. While 30 per cent of hundreds of millions of dollars is still a lot of money, collected in churches and voluntary organizations, it was the governments that ultimately financed relief – without changing their foreign policy.

Pierre Mens
And we should not forget the significance of oil in this context. British Petroleum held a substantial interest in Nigerian oil, and the same was true for the Soviet Union and other nations. The fear of losing access to oil from Nigeria was a prevailing concern.

Lasse Jensen
That is why the French supported the Biafrans.

Pierre Mens
Indeed, but I would also like to raise another point, as we earlier discussed the International Red Cross. I have a clip from November 1968, in which Karl Jaggi, the Swiss representative of the International Red Cross, stated that there was a form of systematic killing and mass slaughter of people in Arba and Asaba.[30] This went beyond isolated incidents; he even went so far as to draw a comparison between the events in Biafra and the atrocities committed by the Germans against the Jews.

Carl Marklund
This refers to a very emotional type of reporting that was prevalent in Western Europe, the idea of Biafra as the "Auschwitz of Africa," a genocidal tragedy that we have not delved into so far. But I would first like to revisit a point you made, Lasse, regarding the similarities and differences between the Vietnam War and the Biafran War in terms of media reporting. In hindsight, it appears that the political mobilization supporting the liberation of South

[30] Karl Heinrich Jaggi, from Switzerland, served as the head of the ICRC delegation in Biafra.

Vietnam was consistently associated with a struggle and fight, and the hope of a success in a sense, despite facing the enormous military apparatus of the United States. This prompts us to consider why the Biafran cause was perceived as so sympathetic on the one hand but deemed so unrealistic on the other. There is some sort of narrative mismatch. Does this line of reasoning resonate?

Lasse Jensen
It does make sense, but it must be viewed against the backdrop of the Cold War. Biafra, the Nigerian Civil War remained detached from the Cold War. We were, not joking, but rather playing with the idea, what if the Soviet Union had supported Biafra? There would have been a massive American intervention in favour of the Federal Military Government. However, the reality was that Biafra existed as an isolated "island" in the Cold War, devoid of direct Cold War influences. The international political support for Biafra was minimal, primarily from a handful of African countries like Tanzania and Gabon, which did not play any significant international role. The only bigger powers that somehow supported Biafra, half-heartedly, were the French and the Chinese.

Carl Marklund
And the Portuguese as well, right?

Lasse Jensen
The Portuguese, of course, and to a certain extent the Spanish, but the Portuguese had self-serving interests. They wanted to safeguard their African colonies. So, there was no Cold War dimension to this country. By contrast, Vietnam represented a quintessential Cold War confrontation with the United States and South Vietnam on one side and North Vietnam, the Liberation Front, the Soviet Union, and to a certain extent China on the other side. It was a clear-cut scenario: the bad guys against the good guys.

Carl Marklund
Easy to organize.

Lasse Jensen
You can decide for yourself who the good guys are. *[Laughter.]*

Carl Marklund
In hindsight.

Lasse Jensen
In Biafra there were no good guys in terms of international politics.

Carl Marklund
Is this your view today or is this the 22-year-old Lasse speaking?

Lasse Jensen
No, no, it is the perspective of the 22-year-old … I grew up with the Cold War, it was a major part of my life. And suddenly I found myself in a region where the Cold War did not play any role. But, of course, I was, we were all sympathetic to the Biafran cause. As I spent time there, to a certain extent, and especially in the years following, I came to realize that it was not a straightforward Igbo national matter, because the eastern region comprised many tribes. The Igbo were the big tribe, but there were numerous other tribes. The "genius" of the federal government was related to this, Gowon's countermeasure: At the moment that the war started, he restructured Nigeria, dissolving the regions and creating twelve states. The Eastern Region was divided into several states, including Calabar and …[31] Because the oil-rich areas were not Igbo areas; they belonged to the Calabar people and there were other tribes.

Carl Marklund
Sorry, I believe Pekka wants to …

[31] On 26 May 1967, Ojukwu decreed to secede from Nigeria; on 27 May 1967, Gowon proclaimed the division of Nigeria into twelve states. This decree split the Eastern Region in three parts: South Eastern State, Rivers State, and East Central State. Three days later, on 30 May 1967, Ojukwu declared Biafran independence, followed by the outbreak of hostilities on 6 July 1967.

Lasse Jensen
It is a complicated thing.

Pekka Peltola
There is also a cultural aspect, which became evident to me, even in my limited experience at a time when I had not been to other places in Africa. Having served in the army, the Finnish army, earlier, I observed deficiencies in the military organization on both the Federal and Biafran sides. While the men were brave, and they went for an attack with perhaps five bullets for their guns, the replenishments and the food supplies mistakenly went the other road. Consequently, everything would collapse, and they would retreat. This occurred frequently on both sides, and the counter-attack just went to nothing. The front line could shift daily over several kilometres, and they did not dig any trenches. Maybe they thought that the enemy would take them and use them. The soldiers just took cover in shallow positions and the bullets were … We could not see, but we could hear bullets, the sharp "tchik" sound they make. And some, of course, also hit people.

All this became clearer to me when I was in Angola, because of the contrast with a more European type of warfare once the Cubans arrived. The Cubans were more open, and they could talk, and so we could better follow how they went forward and actually they also saved us personally sometimes. They possessed much more systematic and appropriate technology and equipment …

Carl Marklund
There was a point you raised earlier, and both you and Lasse delved into this topic. It involves the scenario where you observed both facets of this conflict. Did any of you establish contacts with the Nigerian side when you were there? Or were your operations exclusively confined to the Biafran side?

Pierre Mens
It was impossible to cross the border.

Carl Marklund

I understand that crossing the front line was not possible, but were there instances of humanitarian aid workers or journalists attempting to cover both sides of the conflict?

Lasse Jensen

It was … I mean, when Kissinger talks about the total ineptitude of the federal government in terms of public relations, it also meant that no journalists were allowed into the federal Nigerian side.

Carl Marklund

But that was a Nigerian decision.

Lasse Jensen

That was a Nigerian decision. As a sovereign state, they had the authority to decide whatever they saw fit. But basically, concerning public relations, the Biafrans, along with the churches and the Red Cross, were collectively contributing to covering the Biafran perspective. Covering the other side proved difficult without presence there, and nobody was there. Very few, very few, mainly British journalists were there, but not many. The side that accommodated journalists had a public relation advantage. The side that … The situation might draw a parallel to the limited access Western independent journalists have to the Russian side of the Ukraine conflict. I am not saying that the coverage … I should be very careful to say that the coverage of the Ukraine conflict is slightly Ukrainian biased. But we do not know anything about the other side. Basically, we only know what the propaganda tells us. That is mainly lies, no matter who puts out propaganda.

Carl Marklund

Uno, did you want to add to that?

Uno Grönkvist

Well, yes, I see a similarity with what is happening in Gaza today. Most of the TV teams, journalists, photographers are based in

Israel, receiving abundant information efficiently. In Gaza, there are very few mass media people, mostly Palestinians, Al Jazeera, et cetera. But very, very few. And why? It is impossible to get in there. Work on both sides simultaneously is impossible. And every night you will see *Rapport*, *Aktuellt*, *TV4-Nyheterna*, whatever.[32] The reporters are close to the border to Gaza, but still a few hundred meters on the Israeli side. This leads to one-dimensional reporting from the war, posing a significant problem.

Carl Marklund

Connecting this back to the Biafran situation, looking back now allows us to apply some experiences from the Biafran war to contemporary situations. One crucial aspect is that the Biafrans permitted journalists to enter while experiencing a humanitarian catastrophe. While this was a significant problem for the Biafrans as such, from a media logic, it was an advantage. I am curious because, in your dual roles in humanitarian work and journalism, impartiality is a key principle. Did you reflect on this issue while you were in Biafra, considering that you were mostly reporting from the Biafran side? How did you think about the challenge of impartiality?

Uno Grönkvist

I would personally say, not very much. I was so busy doing my job that I did not reflect that much. Most of my reflections on this war emerged later. I have delved into it afterward, conducted extensive research, and discovered many aspects I neither understood nor was really interested in at the time. Then, I worked tirelessly, sometimes around the clock, to get the right publicity and a good fundraising result. That was my focus.

But nowadays, getting older and older, I find myself reflecting in various ways. Almost every day, as a consumer of news from all

[32] *Rapport* and *Aktuellt* stand as the primary news programs offered by the Swedish public service television broadcaster, Sveriges Television (SVT), while *TV4-Nyheterna* serves as the news program for the private Swedish television channel TV4.

over the world, I contemplate about the conditions of the media. If we shift our focus from Biafra for a moment and look at the TV evening news, what do we observe? A significant portion revolves around events in the United States. Why? Because Swedish TV and radio have reporters stationed in New York City and Washington DC, and they have to do their job. How many reporters cover the fifty-four countries in Africa? Only one, stationed in South Africa. His task is to cover the whole continent, which is impossible. Standing in Johannesburg, he reports on incidents in, let's say Liberia or Mauritania, without being on the scene. He could be stationed in Sweden and provide the same report.

Carl Marklund
Paradoxically, there probably have never been as many Nordic-sourced journalists based in Africa as during the Biafran crisis.

Lasse Jensen
Exactly, exactly.

Carl Marklund
I mean, it was a significant peak of attention focused on Africa and African issues. So, from a Pan-African perspective, I would consider that quite important.

Lasse Jensen
But discussions like these always make you reflect on things you might not have considered. After Biafra, I spent almost a year in Vietnam. And you can say that there, the entire press corps was in South Vietnam. We all had American press cards and were formally recognized as majors in the expeditionary forces in South Vietnam.

Carl Marklund
Speaking of impartiality.

Lasse Jensen

And we were essentially all opponents of the American intervention because we belonged to the '68 generation. However, regardless of how desperately one would try to get to the other side, it remained closed to journalists. During my time in Vietnam, only one Western journalist had ever visited the Viet Cong, the liberated areas of South Vietnam. That reporter was a communist Australian named Wilfred Burchett.[33] And he travelled around; he was the only one, and there were 2,000 of us in South Vietnam.

But the situation in Biafra was different because our involvement was on a humanitarian basis, not on a political basis. As a twenty-two-year-old, when I returned to the agency in Copenhagen and was tasked with writing stories, the first thing I thought was, here we have the Biafran story, here we have the churches story, here we have the Red Cross story – what about the other side? While sitting in Copenhagen writing about it, you would do that. The problem was there was nothing from the other side. Sometimes there was a communique from the military government, and that was about it.

Carl Marklund

Press releases and all.

Lasse Jensen

Press releases. Ultimately, they hired a public relations bureau in New York, which was much less effective than the public relations people the Biafrans had engaged in Geneva. So, it is an interesting – what do you call it – absurdity.

Carl Marklund

Following up on that, you mentioned the openness of the Biafrans – this seems to be the consensus on the panel. However, a sig-

---

[33] Wilfred Graham Burchett (1911–1983), Australian journalist known for being the first Western journalist to report from Hiroshima after the dropping of the atomic bomb, and for his reporting from "the other side" during the wars in Korea and Vietnam.

nificant claim emerged, as we can see with the benefit of hindsight, namely the claim of the Biafrans who portrayed the Nigerians as having genocidal intentions. The blockade of Biafra was seen, if you permit the modern expression, as weaponizing hunger, with the goal being a form of genocide. This became part of the narrative of Biafra as a victim. At the same time, you were treated as guests and had the freedom to travel around in Biafra. How did you perceive this claim of genocide? Did it find reflection in your reports and interactions with the civilian population?

Lasse Jensen
That was part of the Biafran propaganda. Being in Biafra, you tended to believe it. However, as a journalist you maintain scepticism towards such massive claims. And regarding hunger as a weapon, if you delve into classical history, you will know that already the siege of Troy utilized a siege and a blockade to starve out the enemy.

Carl Marklund
Yes, there were also some statements from the Nigerian military …

Lasse Jensen
It is cynical, but there was nothing new in the Nigerian strategy. There are several historical precedents.

Carl Marklund
So, in a way, given the context, it was not entirely implausible, but you were somewhat sceptical?

Lasse Jensen
Well, being in the situation, you might not believe it for 100 per cent, because it did not unfold as claimed. You saw people die from starvation, so it happened in a way. But did that constitute genocide? The fear was that if the Nigerians would win, as they did, they would conduct a genocidal operation, which they did not.

Pekka Peltola
Excuse me, I would like to draw your attention to a novel that, in my opinion, stands out as the by far best novel ever written about the war in Biafra. I am referring to a book by Chimamanda Adichie.[34] It is truly an exceptional novel. While I have received various manuscripts and old books on the subject, Adichie's book surpasses them all. It adeptly navigates the complex situation, incorporating different personal attitudes and other aspects in a masterful way, showcasing her prowess as a writer.

Lasse Jensen
Half of a Yellow Sun.[35] I had the privilege of interviewing her. Adichie shares recollections of the Biafra War in her brilliant book, but these are the stories passed down by her parents and grandparents. So, it has been filtered through. She never experienced anything firsthand because she was just a baby. Was she even born? I don't know.

Carl Marklund
I do not think so.

Lasse Jensen
I believe she was born after the war, actually. A fantastic writer!

Uno Grönkvist
Regarding the topic at hand, it is difficult to tell what is true and what is not true. In my research before this event today, I encountered sources stating one million people died during the Biafra War. Other sources claim three million. That is a big difference in such a small country, or province, whatever you call it, as Biafra.

---

[34] Chimamanda Ngozi Adichie (born 1977) is a distinguished Nigerian author celebrated for her literary contributions, which span novels, short stories, and nonfiction. Recognized as a critically acclaimed young anglophone writer in Nigerian fiction, she has garnered attention on a global scale, notably in her second home, the United States.
[35] Adichie, Chimamanda Ngozi, *Half of a Yellow Sun* (London: Fourth Estate, 2006).

One million or three million – even years after the war, certainty remains elusive.

Carl Marklund
Indeed, true.

Lasse Jensen
It is probably closer to one million.

Uno Grönkvist
Yes, probably, I guess so too.

Susan Lindholm
The issue is also connected to the pre-war history and massacres, where attempts to measure populations in different regions resulted in vastly different numbers.

Lasse Jensen
Simply put, it is incredibly challenging to kill a million people unless it is done on a large scale, like a holocaust.

Susan Lindholm
But listening to you panellists, it appears that your experiences in Biafra and reflections on Biafra are deeply coloured by the starving children, overshadowing other memories. But do these children and the starvation really deserve our sole interest? I would like to ask you again whether there are not any other narratives from that time? We would be really interested in hearing more about that, perhaps about the resistance, or about women … Well, your answer might be that there is nothing.

Uno Grönkvist
To discuss the Red Cross in this context, we had very effective publicity about the events in Biafra for a couple of years, significantly impacting our fundraising results. Either or. The mass media eventually grew tired of reporting in a positive light. So,

they started searching for faults. At the end of the war, they certainly found such a fault. As indicated by some of the pictures during the break while we had biscuits: when we had to halt the flights into Biafra, we still possessed all these aircraft, we had the pilots and had to pay for their salaries, and so on. The *Expressen* newspaper discovered these aircraft that had come back from Biafra parked on an airfield outside Stockholm. They published pictures and conveyed to their readers that these aircraft, bought by the Swedish Red Cross with funds collected through fundraising, were standing there, costing millions of dollars. They declared it a major fiasco and disaster, adopting a negative approach in the end.[36]

Another aspect I have thought of many times is a story that never made it into the Swedish press. The media always seek heroes, right? We had two remarkable heroes in this war, one of them the frequently mentioned Carl Gustaf von Rosen. The other, in my opinion, was Sven Lampell, the head of the Red Cross Air Bridge. He was Rosen's opposite, but also a very colourful personality. He was a colonel, he was a movie star, and he had an impressive background, having worked for the United Nations in Congo, among other roles.

Those two men did significant good during the Biafra War, profoundly affected by what they saw, much like all of us who were there. But what was their conclusion? One chose war, and one peace. Von Rosen became a fighter pilot. He equipped his airplane, as we have heard, with rockets, actively participating in the war. Lampell, on the other hand, decided to leave the Swedish Air Force, although he might have become its head, if he had stayed. But he left this career and joined the International Red Cross in Geneva. He worked as a field delegate, striving for peace in different parts of the world until his retirement. It is quite a story – two heroes, one embracing war, and the other one choosing peace. But no journalist, as far as I know, ever brought these two men together for a discussion.

---

[36] "Så förvaltas våra insamlingspengar: Röda Korsets flyg enorm felsatsning", *Expressen*, 22 Oct. 1969.

Lasse Jensen
That is a good story, a great story.
Uno Grönkvist
It could have been very selling. I don't know why …

Lasse Jensen
You still have time. You do it. *[Laughter]*

Uno Grönkvist
Well, I might have time but unfortunately the two heroes are dead.

Lasse Jensen
I believe the question was whether there were other aspects beyond the starving children.

Susan Lindholm
That is correct.

Lasse Jensen
To me, Biafra was very much about the idea of the children. When I was there, starvation had been somewhat alleviated, although it was still present – there were still a lot of starving children. However, 1968 was the worst year, when you guys were in Biafra *[pointing to the other panellists]*. During my time, 5,000 flights had helped. For my part, I remember distribution problems, certain conflicts between Catholics and Protestants, and spending fifty nights at Uli airfield. I remember the Biafran major, a former headmaster of an elementary school, who still behaved like one and who was the official who handled approvals for flights. I still have my boarding pass, I believe I sent it to you. Most of what we might call the side stories, aside from starvation and disaster, centred around the airlift. That story is why, for thirty years, I wanted to make the film I eventually did about the pilots, the organization, and the successful collaboration among Catholics, Protestants, and Jews,

defying all odds. It all emerged from the back room of a gymnastics exercise hall in Uppsala, way back in '68.[37]

Carl Marklund
It is a fascinating paradox.

Lasse Jensen
There are so many stories that I remember, apart from the starvation.

Carl Marklund
This is exactly what we are after, – understanding that in Biafra the geopolitics of the Cold War did not play a major role, allowing the formation of new alliances. At the same time, at least in Sweden – I do not know whether Uno and Pierre agree with me – it seems as if Biafra was never really a concern for those leaning left. Nevertheless, it was something that really became a very big, non-ideological issue. Maybe that is also why the dominant narrative focused on the cynical but selling story of starving children, which, beyond its obvious truth lacks a deeper exploration of the conflict.

Lasse Jensen
So, it was not that cynical, anyway.

Carl Marklund
Truth is not cynical? Well, maybe.

Pierre Mens
We must not forget that Biafra was in the Eastern Region, which was a rich region with a lot of oil, Port Harcourt, and so on. Nigeria and Gowon were fighting for their life to get back the oil.

---

[37] "Behold, I make all things new": WCC's Fourth Assembly in Uppsala, 4–20 July 1968.

Carl Marklund

Yes, that is a valid point. I think it is time to conclude this segment of the seminar. But, aha, before we do that, let us hear Pierre, and then Uno.

Pierre Mens

I would just like to mention the observer group established in 1968, comprising representatives from Canada, Poland, Sweden, the United Kingdom, the Organization of African Unity (OAU), and the United Nations.[38] They did their job, but only in 1970 came their final report.[39] This group was not allowed to visit Aba because the road was in a bad condition, instead they were guided to other places far away from Aba. They did not look for the mass graves. This group faced harsh international criticism. Von Rosen said about them that it was a mistake to choose military professional killers as observers.

Carl Marklund

Thank you, Pierre, for your important clarification. Uno, would you like to add something?

Uno Grönkvist

I can think of one thing. I watched the TV news in Sweden yesterday about the Swedish football fans who were killed in Brussels. On the same day, there was an attack on a hospital in Gaza, with an estimated five hundred dead human beings, maybe even more. When the TV news started last night, the first report was about

---

[38] Against the background of the intense Biafran accusations against the Federal Government and its troops for committing or intending to commit genocide against the Biafran population, the Federal Government decided on 28 August 1968 to issue invitations to the governments of Sweden, Canada, Poland and the United Kingdom as well as to the UN and OAU Secretaries General to appoint an observer to be part of an international observer group, which would accompany the federal troops to report any abuses against the civilian population.

[39] The international observer group delivered a series of interim reports and special reports, the final report being delivered in February 1970.

the two Swedes killed in Brussels, and only later, after about ten to fifteen minutes, there was coverage of what happened in Gaza. Two Swedes against five hundred Palestinians.

Why were Swedish journalists so interested, for such a long time, in the Biafra War? They grew rather tired of the starving children; they could not sustain the coverage only based on them. The answer is, there were so many Swedes involved: Swedish pilots, a high number of Swedish relief workers on the ground. Several of them died, passed away. First, there was a Swedish aircraft that crashed, with a Swedish crew aboard, and all of them died. Then there was the front line where Nigerian troops crossed. We had Swedish posts there. One Swedish doctor, a doctor from Yugoslavia, and two missionaries were killed. And a couple of other Swedish relief workers were injured. And then, finally, we had the shootdown of the Swedish Red Cross aircraft. Everyone aboard that aircraft was Swedish, and all of them died. There were big headlines. So, I would say one of the reasons is that from the Danish point, from the Finnish point, and from the Swedish point of view, all the citizens involved in our country were affected.

Susan Lindholm
That is a highly interesting reflection. It is now time to let the audience ask their questions.

Norbert Götz
May I ask the opening question, directed perhaps to Lasse. Like many others, I have a curiosity in the Swedish figure, Carl Gustaf von Rosen. Various narratives exist, but essentially his dismissal as a chief of Nordchurchaid stemmed from blending humanitarian and military aid. Later, he was noted for conducting raids into Nigeria, as witnessed by Pierre. However, my examination of archival documents gives the impression that his relationships with churches remained good. Did von Rosen sustain positive connections with the churches? Were they informed about the developments, and did they anticipate the course of events? I would appreciate your insights on this aspect.

Pierre Mens
I believe Carl Gustaf von Rosen had a positive relationship. In Sweden, he was somewhat of a hero due to his actions. Even in Ethiopia, he maintained a very good reputation despite the change of government to Mengistu Haile Mariam.[40] Von Rosen later flew food into Ethiopia, "bombed" with food in small villages that could not be reached by Land Rovers or so.

Norbert Götz
Thank you. Lasse, do you disagree?

Lasse Jensen
No, I conducted extensive research for my film, including in-depth discussions with Viggo Mollerup, the head of Nordchurchaid, and Father Byrne, who led Caritas. As mentioned, Byrne and Viggo were the two bosses of the airlift. Von Rosen was never the boss of the airlift, he served as the chief of flight operations.

Norbert Götz
Yes, that is exactly what I meant.

Lasse Jensen
Which meant he was the chief pilot. He was fired because, in press conferences, he became increasingly militant in his support for Biafra. I have not heard allegations that von Rosen was smuggling arms into Biafra with church planes, and I believe it is not true, given the strict controls in São Tomé at the time.

However, when he was fired, it was simply because he had crossed the line. The churches, while assisting the Biafrans, that was like the nature of things, were cautious not to take a political stand in terms of Biafra versus FMG, the Federal Military Government. Von Rosen was simply dismissed from one day to the next

---

[40] Mengistu Haile Mariam b. 1937 is an Ethiopian former politician and former army officer who was the head of state of Ethiopia from 1977 to 1991 and General Secretary of the Workers' Party of Ethiopia from 1984 to 1991.

and expelled from São Tomé. After that, there were no cordial relations between Nordchurchaid and von Rosen.

I was present when he initiated the bombing with the mini-coins. Interestingly, do you know why it is called coins and not mini-cons? No? C-O-I-N, Mini Counter Insurgency Aircraft. He introduced the concept of guerrilla warfare in the air. However, he had then crossed the line, and from the churches' perspective, he was no longer useful to them, having jeopardized their efforts. I recall they were very worried when the MFI started flying.[41]

Norbert Götz
Okay, thank you. Yes, at least that is the official version.

Lasse Jensen
It is also the unofficial version from people I am talking to.

Norbert Götz
I pass the microphone over for the next question to Gloria Chuku.

Gloria Chuku
Thank you very much, panellists. I have three questions. The first one is how the multinational foreigners who worked in Biafra coordinated the activities of airlifting and the distribution of relief materials in Biafra. I think, Lasse, you mentioned, the fact that you were free moving around. And the question that comes to mind is if this was due to pre-screening before you flew into Biafra? Were the Biafran authorities assured that aircraft coming in either from São Tomé or Gabon had already been screened, therefore alleviating concerns about potential spies? I am curious how all these various groups worked, outside Biafra and within Biafra.

My second question concerns Lasse's reference to genocide as Biafran propaganda. My question is, on what basis do you make this

---

[41] Malmö Flygindustri (MFI) was a small aviation and car company in south Sweden which specialized in small single-propeller aircraft and various plastic objects. It was later acquired by SAAB. Von Rosen's aircraft were purchased from MFI.

comment or assertion? Is it based on the number of people who died or on the postwar declaration by Gowon that there would be "no victor, no vanquished"? Does such a declaration offset the fact that it was a federal government policy to use starvation as a weapon of war? Could we use what happened after the war to nullify the fear that Biafrans had that they were going to suffer mass execution or elimination?

My last point concerns the repeated question about alternative stories. I am surprised that I did not hear anything about the resilience of Biafrans, especially about Biafran women, participating in the distribution of relief materials and serving in other capacities, including at refugee camps, and thereby ensuring that about five million survived the war. Could you have been affected by your gender in reporting about the Biafra War and by ignoring the role of Biafran women in sustaining the war? The pre-war population of Biafra was eleven million, and after the war it was five million. I am not suggesting that six million died, although I have some questions surrounding the leaning towards one million instead of three million who were killed. Is there any justification or any sources supporting the lower number vis-a-vis the higher number of the dead?

I am just wondering whether there was a conscious effort to suppress the resilience of Biafrans and emphasize their suffering, and the famine and starvation. Was this a strategy to touch on the conscience and sympathy of the public in order to mobilize for the aid effort? Perhaps, presenting another image and the resilience of Biafrans may not have motivated more people to support the relief effort. But it would have been valuable, at least after the war, to present more balanced accounts. Thank you very much.

Lasse Jensen

These are three challenging questions. Firstly, regarding the organization inside Biafra, it was structured according to the aid organizations involved. The Red Cross, Caritas, and the World Council of Churches each had their own logistical setups, refugee centres, and distribution systems, including lorries, petrol deliveries, and all that. By and large, that worked miraculously. Organization took very much place within the three distinct contexts, although the Red Cross had disappeared when I was based in Biafra. Anyhow, the two church consortia each had their separate organization and there was not much cooperation between Caritas and the WCC inside Biafra.

With regard to the second question, that regarding genocide, I would like to point to something I found during my research that is not generally known. We can reasonably assert that genocide did not occur after the conclusion of the war. One contributing factor was a lesser-known airlift organized by the US government. I believe it started a week after the end of the war. By mid-January 1970, large US Air Force planes, with nationality marks painted over on request by the Nigerians, brought in thousands of tons of relief.[42] We will never know whether that was distributed rightly, and we never knew in Nigeria at the time, for several reasons. However, it served as a signal from the US government to the Nigerian government, urging restraint and discouraging violence against Igbos or Biafrans. This signal seemingly had an impact, or the federal military government genuinely meant it when they said they intended to avoid retributions.

Concerning the population figures ranging from five to eleven million, the discrepancy may arise from distinguishing between the eleven million in the Eastern Region and the five million in the East Central State, the Igbo heartland, which became a separate state. Including the other three states, River State, Cala-

---

[42] The official history of the post-war humanitarian operations of the USAF Military Airlift Command summarizes this as follows: "On January 12, President Nixon offered aid to Nigeria for the refugees. The Nigerian government, having already received many food shipments from other countries, requested an airlift of other relief cargo, including hospital equipment, blankets, and trucks to transport food and refugees. […] Between January 27 and February 10, the six airplanes airlifted more than 436 tons of relief cargo to Nigeria." Daniel L. Haulman, *The United States Air Force and Humanitarian Airlift Operations 1947–1994* (Washington, D.C.: Air Force Historical Research Agency, 1998), 305.

bar and so on, the total might be around ten million, but this is speculative.

Norbert Götz
I believe we can have one or two more questions before wrapping up.

William Sharman
I will keep it brief. I have a comment and then a question. Regarding the point about aid being non-ideological, I would just say it was perceived as such. The effort did stand for something significant, as reflected in the novel you mentioned, which begins with people arguing about the country's ideology.

Lasse Jensen
I meant non-ideological in the Cold War context.

William Sharman
Right, I understand.

Lasse Jensen
Communism versus …

William Sharman
Right, my question is, I am not aware of any other cases where a conflict in Europe or elsewhere in the world resonated so strongly in Scandinavian countries. Why do you think this particular conflict had such a profound impact in Scandinavia.

Norbert Götz
We will take the next question right away. Please, Martin.

Martin Johansson
I will try to be brief. First, I would like to echo what Bill mentioned about the ideological aspects. I understand you meant the Cold War perspective, but from what I gather, there were significant ideo-

logical concerns – not least in the Swedish press material on von Rosen's mission accompanied by Pierre, involving arms smuggling. The Biafran cause was undoubtedly sellable to a Swedish media audience, if not necessarily from a Cold War standpoint.

My question is about gender. Firstly, about your gender. You were all men, and from what I understand, this entire operation was a very male one. Pilots, aid workers, journalists – practically everyone involved was male. Pekka, you mentioned that your wife was at São Tomé, but that was an exception. It appears to have been a distinctly masculine environment, which is not always the case in humanitarian work. In some spheres of society, everyone tends to be male, but that is not typical in this field.

So, why was it an all-male environment in Biafra, and how do you believe it affected your work? Also, how did it influence the narratives you presented? We discussed what is sellable and what is not, and there were very few women in the stories. This, once again, is not always the case. Do you think that this highly masculine environment of the airlift, including journalists and pilots, impacted your ability or possibility to connect with women and convey their stories? If not, do you have any other explanation for the absence of women in the narratives at that time?

Norbert Götz
Who would like to respond to these two questions?

Lasse Jensen
Well, I know that in 2023 this means navigating some tricky terrain. *[Laughter.]* No, I get your question.

Martin Johansson
You might say it is not observable; I buy that.

Lasse Jensen
Hey, the world in 1968 was a predominantly masculine world. Journalism, especially foreign journalism, was almost entirely male, with a few exceptional women reporters, but they were very

few. It was a male-dominated profession. Pilots? I cannot recall any female pilots from that time, except for Amelia Earhart.[43]

So, in a way, this masculine environment was pervasive. The airlift was masculine because the pilots were men. In the church hierarchy, obviously in the Catholic hierarchy, there were very few women priests, actually none. In the Protestant environment of that time, there were very few women leaders. I can think of one woman, Mona Mollerup, whom I did a story about many years later. She was the wife of Viggo Mollerup and a driving force in Nordchurchaid, more or less its administrative head. She is Canadian, multilingual, and still alive and kicking. But in 1968, '69, '70, it was a masculine world, and that dominated everything.

Susan Lindholm

But there were nuns and also the women Gloria mentioned, the local women who played a crucial role in helping people survive. So, it is just that their narratives did not make it to the forefront.

Lasse Jensen

I am not saying there were not any women; there were millions of women. But were there women who played a significant role in what journalists are interested in – hierarchy, power, organization, and so forth? And in that sense, it seemed natural at the time.

Norbert Götz

We need to pick up the pace a bit, but Uno and then Pekka, and then we have to quickly move to the concluding statements.

Uno Grönkvist

A brief response to your question. I was not initially supposed to be in Biafra at all. Our news magazine had a female editor who was selected to go there. Just a few days before her departure, my boss, the secretary general, told me, "You better go". And I asked, "Why?" The explanation was that, at that time, I was single. She was a divorced woman, mother to a child of seven or eight. And

[43] Amelia Earhart (1897–1937) was a US aviation pioneer.

he said, "It's very risky. It's not sure you will get back. It's better that you go, rather than Kerstin" – that was her name.

Norbert Götz
Pekka.

Pekka Peltola
Perhaps I am repeating myself, but I recall more vividly now. My first trip was towards the end of August. There was one woman, I believe she was a Dutch journalist, around fifty or sixty years old, and I am not certain if she was actually permitted to enter Biafra. She was the only woman. Then next time, a month later, when I came with my wife, there was one more lady involved, and that was the wife of von Rosen, and nobody else. My wife, von Rosen's wife, and one, possibly Danish or Swedish, journalist a month prior.

Norbert Götz
Thank you. Now, I believe we will give you the floor once again for a final statement of about two or three minutes. So, let's start with you, Pekka.

Pekka Peltola
Well, first of all, I am flattered that I have been invited here on account of some of my stories from fifty-five years ago. The audience should be aware that an occasion when somebody wants to know from you what you think about something and what you wrote about something fifty-five years ago is a great honour. I appreciate it very much. Watching the film that I produced again, my conviction was confirmed that when a person is twenty-seven, twenty-eight, twenty-nine, he or she is in the height of his or her thinking and acting age. So, thank you very much for the invitation.

Susan Lindholm
Thank you for being with us. Thank you very much.

Uno Grönkvist

I would like to share a quotation and a reflection, both within the time limit. Firstly, the quotation: "From a media point of view, Biafra was a success story. [...] But from a humanitarian point of view, it was an operational disaster, a logistical nightmare and a political failure." This quote is sourced from the article "Humanitarian Aid and the Biafra War: Lessons not Learned,"[44] published by the Council for the Development of Social Science Research in Africa in 2009, and I do agree with this judgement. Almost everyone could realize early on that the breakaway state of Biafra would never be able to defeat Nigeria. How would the situation have evolved without rescue operations – might thousands and thousands of lives have been saved? What is right and what is wrong? Nobody knows. But as far as I know, the media did not raise this important question as long as the Biafra War lasted, at least not in Sweden.

Lasse Jensen

I have not prepared a final statement, and I believe I have talked enough. I will join Pekka expressing my gratitude for the invitation. About eight or ten years ago, I believed I had concluded my involvement with Biafra. As a young journalist, I dedicated years and years to this cause, later producing a film and talking to dozens of people, including pilots and church representatives. It became a significant part of my life, and I genuinely believed I was done with it. However, upon receiving your email, I found myself engaged once again, spending a month digging into my archives and suddenly recalling many things I thought I had forgotten – thank you for that.

Norbert Götz

Thank you for sharing with us.

---

[44] Marc-Antoine Pérouse de Montclos, "Humanitarian Aid and the Biafra War: Lessons not Learned," *Africa Development* 34 (2009) 1: 69–82.

Pierre Mens

Today, a situation akin to Biafra would no longer occur. Due to technical developments, all the church aid airplanes would be shot down by heat-seeking missiles, even von Rosen's mini-coins. The United Nations is much stronger today than it was then, and we have NATO and the EU, and consider what that cohesion means in Ukraine. So today, England, Russia, and former East Germany would not be able to sell weapons in exchange for oil and other goods. The highly questionable Gowon regime would not have survived for long. Despite all this, famine is still being used as a weapon. This is evident in the Tigray conflict, where Ethiopia for a long time refused aid. We have Israel, which, after Hamas' horrific attack, refuses to release water, electricity, and necessities to North Gaza. Unfortunately, I think we will continue to face terror, not the least in Africa.

Carl Marklund

Many thanks to our four panellists for generously sharing your experiences and perspectives on the situation in Biafra some fifty years ago. It has been a pleasure to take part in this insightful conversation, and I thank you very much for having come here, visited us, and engaged with us. Special gratitude goes to our audience and our esteemed guests, Gloria Chuku and Bill Sharman, for joining us. We greatly appreciate your presence. Additionally, I want to express my thanks to Gustav Almestad and the recording team from Södertörn Universitys library, whose technical expertise made this event possible. With these words, I would like to bring the workshop to a close. Thank you all. And a special thank you to my colleague Susan as well!

Susan Lindholm

Thank you, Carl! *[Applause.]*

References

Adichie, Chimamanda Ngozi, *Half of a Yellow Sun* (London: Fourth Estate, 2006).

"Daring Airlift Director; Henry Arthur Warton," *New York Times*, 30 July 1968.

Forsyth, Frederick, *The Biafra Story* (Harmondsworth: Penguin, 1969).

Götz, Norbert, "Towards Expressive Humanitarianism: The Formative Experience of Biafra", *An Era of Value Change: The Seventies in Europe*, ed. by Fiammetta Balestracci, Christina von Hodenberg, and Isabel Richter (Oxford: Oxford University Press, forthcoming 2024), 207–232.

Götz, Norbert, Georgina Brewis, & Steffen Werther, *Humanitarianism in the Modern World: The Moral Economy of Famine Relief* (Cambridge: Cambridge University Press, 2020).

Götz, Norbert & Irène Herrmann, "Universalism in Emergency Aid before and after 1970: Ambivalences and Contradictions", *Nationalism and Internationalism Intertwined: A European History of Concepts Beyond the Nation State*, ed. by Pasi Ihalainen and Antero Holmila (New York: Berghahn, 2022), 247–269.

Haulman, Daniel L., *The United States Air Force and Humanitarian Airlift Operations 1947–1994* (Washington, D.C.: Air Force Historical Research Agency, 1998).

Hofgren, Alan (ed.), *Haile Selassies land: Ett bildverk om svenskarnas insatser i Etiopien* (Stockholm: Ev. fosterl.-stift., 1961).

Hofgren, Allan (ed.), *Tanganyika: Ett bildverk om svenska insatser i Afrika* (Stockholm: Förlaget Filadelfia, 1963).

Marklund, Carl, *Neutrality and Solidarity in Nordic Humanitarian Action* (London: Overseas Development Institute, 2016).

Marklund, Carl, "From Unconditional Solidarity to Conditional Evaluability: Competing Notions of Conditionality and the Swedish Aid Model," in Antoine de Bengy Puyvallée and Kristian Bjørkdahl (eds.), *Do-Gooders at the End of Aid: Scandinavian Humanitarianism in the 21st Century* (Cambridge: Cambridge University Press, 2021), 171-193.

Marklund, Carl, "The Moral Diplomacy of Decolonisation: Swedish Responses to the Rising Global South, 1950s-1970s," in *Economia & Lavoro*, Anno LV, 2 (2021), 35–57.

Memorandum: The White House, Washington, Tuesday, January 28, 1969, Memorandum for the President from: Henry A. Kissinger, Subject: U. S. Options in Biafra Relief, Foreign Relations, 1969-1976, Volume E-5, Documents on Africa, 1969–1972. https://2001-2009.state.gov/r/pa/ho/frus/nixon/e5/55258.htm.

Møller-Rasmussen, Lars, *Presse og magt: Manipulation og fordrejning i mediernes nyhedsdækning* (København: Gyldendal, 1972).

Pérouse de Montclos, Marc-Antoine, "Humanitarian Aid and the Biafra War: Lessons not Learned," *Africa Development* 34 (2009) 1: 69–82.

"Så förvaltas våra insamlingspengar: Röda Korsets flyg enorm felsatsning", *Expressen*, 22 Oct. 1969.

Slotnik, Daniel E., "Lloyd Garrison, 83, Journalist; Covered Africa for The Times," *New York Times*, 1 July 2014.

Issues of Contemporary History / Samtidshistoriska frågor

This series is published by The Institute of Contemporary History (Samtidshistoriska institutet, SHI). The series summarizes and discusses significant historical events and contemporary issues. Edited transcripts from witness seminars, new research from the university's academic staff and conference reports are published as part of the series. Information about the series: https://bibl-app.sh.se/publicationseries/list?id=12.

Most of the titles in the series can be downloaded in full text, free of charge, from the Digital Science Archive, DiVA, http://www.diva-portal.se.

Some of the titles in the series are published in collaboration with the Center for Baltic and East European Studies (CBEES) at Södertörn University. Responsible for the work with the publication series is Professor Norbert Götz, norbert.gotz@sh.se.

1. *Olof Palme i sin tid.* Ed. Kjell Östberg (2001).
2. *Kvinnorörelsen och '68.* Ed. Elisabeth Elgán (2001).
3. *Riv alla murar! Vittnesseminarier om sexliberalismen och om Pockettidningen R.* Ed. Lena Lennerhed (2002).
4. *Löntagarfonderna – en missad möjlighet?* Ed. Lars Ekdahl (2002).
5. *Dagens Nyheter: Minnesseminarium över Sven-Erik Larsson. Vittnesseminarium om DN och '68.* Ed. Alf W. Johansson (2003).
6. *Kvinnorna skall göra det! Den kvinnliga medborgarskolan på Fogelstad – som idé, text och historia.* Eds. Ebba Witt Brattström & Lena Lennerhed (2003).
7. *Moderaterna, marknaden och makten – svensk högerpolitik under avregleringens tid, 1976–1991.* Torbjörn Nilsson (2003).

8. *Upprorets estetik. Vittnesseminarier om kulturens politisering under 1960- och 1970-talet.* Ed. Lena Lennerhed (2005).

9. *Revolution på svenska – ett vittnesseminarium om jämställdhetens institutionalisering, politisering och expansion 1972–1976.* Ed. Anja Hirdman (2005).

10. *En högskola av ny typ? Två seminarier kring Södertörns högskolas tillkomst och utveckling.* Eds. Mari Gerdin & Kjell Östberg (2006).

11. *Hur rysk är den svenska kommunismen? Fyra bidrag om kommunism, nationalism och etnicitet.* Eds. Mari Gerdin & Kjell Östberg (2006).

12. *Ropen skalla – daghem åt alla! Vittnesseminarium om daghemskampen på 70-talet.* Eds. Mari Gerdin & Kajsa Ohrlander (2007).

13. *Makten i kanslihuset. Vittnesseminarium 16 maj 2006.* Eds. Emma Isaksson & Torbjörn Nilsson (2007).

14. *Partnerskapslagen – ett vittnesseminarium om partnerskapslagens tillkomst.* Eds. Emma Isaksson & Lena Lennerhed (2007).

15. *Vägar till makten – statsrådens och statssekreterarnas karriärvägar.* Anders Ivarsson Westerberg & Cajsa Niemann (2007).

16. *Sverige och Baltikums frigörelse. Två vittnesseminarier om storpolitik kring Östersjön 1991–1994.* Eds. Thomas Lundén & Torbjörn Nilsson (2008).

17. *Makten och trafiken i Stadshuset. Två vittnesseminarier om Stockholms kommunalpolitik.* Ed. Torbjörn Nilsson (2009).

18. *Norden runt i tvåhundra år. Jämförande studier om liberalism, konservatism och historiska myter.* Torbjörn Nilsson (2010).

19. *1989 med svenska ögon. Vittnesseminarium om Östeuropas omvandling.* Eds. Torbjörn Nilsson & Thomas Lundén (2010).

20. *Statsminister Göran Persson i samtal med Erik Fichtelius (1996–2006).* Ed. Werner Schmidt (2011).

21. *Bortom rösträtten. Politik, kön och medborgarskap i Norden.* Eds. Lenita Freidenwall & Josefin Rönnbäck (2011).

22. *Borgerlig fyrklöver intog Rosenbad – regeringsskiftet 1991.* Eds. Torbjörn Nilsson & Anders Ivarsson Westerberg (2011).

23. *Rivstart för Sverige – Alliansen och maktskiftet 2006.* Eds. Fredrik Eriksson & Anders Ivarsson Westerberg (2012).

24. *Det började i Polen – Sverige och Solidaritet 1980–1981.* Ed. Fredrik Eriksson (2013).

25. *Förnyelse eller förfall? Svenska försvaret efter kalla kriget*. Ed. Fredrik Eriksson (2013).

26. *Staten och granskningssamhället*. Eds. Bengt Jacobsson & Anders Ivarsson Westerberg (2013).

27. *Almedalen – varför är vi här? Så skapades en politikens marknadsplats – Ett vittnesseminarium om Almedalsveckan som politisk arena*. Ed. Kjell Östberg (2013).

28. *Anarkosyndikalismens återkomst i Spanien. SACs samarbete med CNT under övergången från diktatur till demokrati*. Ed. Per Lindblom (2014).

29. *När blev vården marknad? Vittnesseminarium i Almedalen*. Ed. Kristina Abiala (2014).

30. *Brinner "förorten"? Om sociala konflikter i Botkyrka och Huddinge*. Ed. Kristina Abiala (2014).

31. *Sea of Identities: A Century of Baltic and East European Experiences with Nationality, Class, and Gender*. Ed. Norbert Götz (2014).

32. *När räntan gick i taket: Vittnesseminarium om valutakrisen 1992*. Ed. Cecilia Åse (2015).

33. *Nordiskt samarbete i kalla krigets kölvatten. Vittnesseminarium med Uffe Ellemann-Jensen, Mats Hellström och Pär Stenbäck*. Eds. Johan Strang & Norbert Götz (2016).

34. *Solidariteten med Chile 1973–1989*. Eds. Yulia Gradskova & Monica Quirico (2016).

35. *25 år av skolreformer – hur började det? Vittnesseminarium om skolans kommunalisering och friskolereformen*. Ed. Johanna Ringarp (2017).

36. *Levande campus: Utmaningar och möjligheter för Södertörns högskola i den nya regionala stadskärnan i Flemingsberg*. Eds. Johanna Ringarp & Håkan Forsell (2017).

37. *Utbildningsvetenskap: Vittnesseminarium om ett vetenskapsområdes uppkomst, utveckling och samtida utmaningar*. Eds. Anders Burman, Daniel Lövheim & Johanna Ringarp (2018).

38. *Pontus Hultén på Moderna Museet: Vittnesseminarium på Södertörns högskola, 26 april 2017*. Eds. Charlotte Bydler, Andreas Gedin & Johanna Ringarp (2018).

39. *AIDS i Sverige: Hivepidemin och rörelserna*. Eds. Kjell Östberg & Lena Lennerhed (2019).

40. *Romerna och skolplikten: Hot eller möjlighet?* Ed. Håkan Blomqvist (2020).

41. *Sweden in Solidarity, Museums in Exile: The Chilean Resistance Museum in Solidarity with Salvador Allende and the International Art Exhibition for Palestine.* Ed. Charlotte Bydler (2022).

42. *Kamp mot droger: En bok om Förbundet mot droger.* Kjell Östberg (2019).

43. *North and South: European Social Democracy in the 1970s.* Eds. Alan Granadino, Carl Marklund & Johan Strang (2021).

44. *Recollections of Joining the EU: Iberian and Nordic Experiences.* Eds. Alan Granadino, Peter Stadius & Carl Marklund (2023).

45. *Visions of the Nordic Model in Northern and Southern Europe (1970s–1990s).* Eds. Alan Granadino, Andreas Mørkved Hellenes & Carl Marklund (2023).

46. *Sverigebilden i USA: Historia, händelser och mekanismer.* Carl Marklund (2023).

47. *The Image of Sweden in the USA: History, Events and Mechanisms.* Carl Marklund (2024).

48. *Biafra and the Nordic Media.* Eds. Norbert Götz & Carl Marklund (2024).